"This timely and accessible book will inspire and encourage Christians everywhere to persevere in their marathon race to future glory. Above all it exhorts us to fix our eyes on the Lord Jesus, who is the only hero who can save us and who has set us the supreme example to follow."

JOHN STEVENS, National Director, Fellowship of Independent Evangelical Churches (FIEC)

"After over 30 years in Christian ministry, Richard Coekin understands the Bible, his local church and the culture. He sees the need for Christians to internalise the great chapter on faith, Hebrews 11, in order to have the resilience they'll need in a culture that is increasingly hostile. An incredibly timely book."

RICO TICE, Senior Minister (Evangelism), All Souls Langham Place, London; Co-founder, Christianity Explored Ministries

"This book inspired me to stop faffing around and to live out my faith whatever the cost as I wait for the glorious future that Christ has won for me. I pray it does the same for you."

LIZZY SMALLWOOD, London Women's Convention

"The author of this book says that to live without faith is to live not at all. Each chapter vividly unfolds as if one were looking at a painting. This age we live in is as fierce, sharp and dangerous for many Christians as the time of the writer of Hebrews. So, this book is desperately needed."

NAM JOON KIM, Pastor, Yullin Church, Korea

"This book on Hebrews 11 is not only gripping to read; it is also simultaneously deeply encouraging and challenging. It is thoughtful and well-illustrated, and packed with gold!"

WILLIAM TAYLOR, Rect'

D1350348

"This book is another example of Richard's passion and refreshing ability to make the Bible come alive. In a world of celebrities, it is so important for every Christian to understand that God uses ordinary people—people who are largely unnoticed in the affairs of the world—to accomplish his eternal purposes. If you find yourself tired or discouraged in serving God, this is the book for you! I cannot recommend it more highly!"

MARTIN MORRISON, Pastor, Christ Church Midrand, Johannesburg, SA; Chairman, The Gospel Coalition, Africa

"A gem of a book that will build and strengthen the church. Achingly relevant, heartwarming, challenging and inspiring— the perfect antidote for my pandemic-weary faith."

LINDA ALLCOCK, Author, *Head, Heart, Hands* and *Deeper Still*

"This is a book written to encourage and refresh. It does that but also much more. By stepping us through the pastorally rich drama of Hebrews 11, this book has the power to transform and change a life—in a good way! It is the product of decades of teaching the Bible to real people dealing with real issues in the real world. It is engaging, pastorally sensitive, thoughtful, provocative and timely. Just what we need."

ANDREW HEARD, Senior Minister, EV Church, New South Wales; Chairman, Australian FIEC

"A delightful book, seasoned with pastoral wisdom and personal experience, peppered with well-chosen illustrations, encouraging Christians under pressure everywhere to live and speak and love with salty faith."

JOHNNY JUCKES, President, Oak Hill College, London

RICHARD COEKIN

FAITH
for
LIFE

thegoodbook
COMPANY

This book is dedicated to my dear friend

DAVE CLARKE
(1963 – 2020)

who lived by faith and went home early.

"I have fought the good fight, I have finished the race,
I have kept the faith." (2 Timothy 4 v 7)

You talked constantly of the joy of being with Jesus in heaven,
which made you such a wonderfully encouraging man to be
with and which motivated your investment in so much gospel
ministry, beginning with your inspirational family. I miss you,
mate—but look forward to seeing you soon.

Faith for Life
Inspiration From The Ordinary Heroes Of Hebrews 11
© Richard Coekin 2021.

Published by:
The Good Book Company

thegoodbook.com | thegoodbook.co.uk
thegoodbook.com.au | thegoodbook.co.nz | thegoodbook.co.in

Unless indicated, all Scripture references are taken from the Holy Bible, New
International Version. Copyright © 2011 Biblica, Inc.TM Used by permission.

All emphasis in Scripture quotations have been added by the author.

ISBN: 9781784986186 | Printed in the UK

Design by André Parker

CONTENTS

PREFACE

In April 2019 I stood among huge, jostling crowds lining the Embankment in London amidst a cacophony of noise. I was there to cheer my son along as he ran the London Marathon with a friend to raise support for disadvantaged kids.

It wasn't the elite athletes who were most impressive—bounding along like speedy gazelles. It was the charity runners—staggering around the 26-mile course from Blackheath to Buckingham Palace for countless great causes, often in ridiculous costumes. It was so humbling to watch their commitment. And moving to hear their supporters bellowing encouragements with all manner of horns and rattles and whistles. And what was motivating the colossal effort of so many thousands of ordinary runners? The finishing line! The satisfaction of completing the course; the triumph of collecting a winner's medal; the joy of helping some people in need. Unsurprisingly, it's the support of the crowds that apparently keeps exhausted runners going through the inevitable muscle and joint fatigue, dehydration and "hitting the wall".

The London Marathon serves as a metaphor for the Christian life. For, while it's an incredible privilege to know God through Jesus, Christians get weary, face opposition and feel discouraged. We certainly want the everlasting satisfaction, triumph and joy of the finish line in heaven. But the personal disappointment of apparently unanswered prayers, the increasingly fierce opposition of Western "identity politics" or the costly grind of commitment to our local church can suck the joy out of us—and sometimes we just feel like giving up. Like those London Marathon runners, we need the support of our spiritual family and friends as they rally around and cheer us on.

There's one spectacular chapter in the Bible through which our Father in heaven does this more wonderfully than any other. It's the famous Hebrews chapter 11— often described as the Bible's "Hall of Fame" (though, as we'll see, it's much more besides).

This amazing portion of Scripture offers powerful encouragements for weary, beleaguered and discouraged Christians. It's like that crowd lining the London Embankment: characters from Bible history, many generations of our spiritual family, who have all completed the course themselves, cheering us on. They manage our expectations with refreshing honesty in a world of lies and spin. They remind us of the glory and blessing that await us at the finishing line in the kindness of God and the happiness of heaven. They inspire us to keep living by faith in the gospel—to endure through the exhaustion, opposition and discouragement that we will all face at some time. They really can encourage us to keep going.

This book is the distillation of many years of teaching this extraordinary chapter to ordinary Christian believers in need of refreshment. It could be ideal for private devotional reading—or perhaps as holiday reading. It could be a timely gift for a discouraged Christian friend, or as background reading to a series of small-group studies in Hebrews 11.

However you use this book, my prayer is that God will graciously use it to encourage and empower you to keep running—living by faith in the promises of God and empowered by faith—for life.

INTRODUCING THE HEBREWS

Shrinking back from living by faith

Remember those earlier days after you received the light, when you endured in a great conflict full of suffering. Sometimes you were publicly exposed to insult and persecution; at other times you stood side by side with those who were so treated. You suffered along with those in prison and joyfully accepted the confiscation of your property, because you knew that you yourselves had better and lasting possessions. So do not throw away your confidence; it will be richly rewarded.

You need to persevere so that when you have done the will of God, you will receive what he has promised. For, "In just a little while, he who is coming will come and will not delay." And, "But my righteous one will live by faith. And I take no pleasure in the one who shrinks back."

But we do not belong to those who shrink back and are destroyed, but to those who have faith and are saved.

(Hebrews 10 v 32-39)

When my wife and I visited Marrakesh in Morocco a few years ago, in one of the bustling *souks* we discovered a pile of wooden crates full of chameleons. As you probably know, chameleons are amazing lizards. By controlling the bloodflow to their skin, they can adapt their colouration to become camouflaged against any background so as to be invisible and safe from predators.

It struck me that Christians can easily become afflicted with what we might call the "chameleon syndrome". Jesus plainly said:

> If anyone is ashamed of me and my words in this
> adulterous and sinful generation, the Son of Man
> [Jesus] will be ashamed of them when he comes in
> his Father's glory.   (Mark 8 v 38)

Christians should not be hiding their faith. We should not become spiritual chameleons: desperately trying to fit into the culture of this world to remain camouflaged and safe from predators who might expose and condemn our faith. But many of us are under immense pressure to do just that.

Perhaps we used to be distinctively Christian—holding to our biblical convictions and looking for opportunities to be respectfully evangelistic. But now we're wary, anxious or even afraid of being discovered. And nobody on our building site or hospital ward or in our college class or city office would ever guess we were a Christian. We've become camouflaged—like chameleons—shrinking back from public loyalty to Christ.

There are many reasons why Christians hide their faith. It could be because of a weariness verging on cynicism after years of social rejection for following Jesus. Or it may be that during the Covid-19 pandemic, with churches unable to meet physically and ministries forced online, while more outsiders have been watching church on YouTube, others of us have quietly drifted away. Or it may be the stress of keeping our jobs where we're bound by official or unofficial codes of conduct that inhibit or even forbid sharing our faith. Whatever the reasons, many who were once openly Christian will be tempted to hide, to shrink back from distinctive Christian living except on Sundays, becoming indistinguishable from unbelievers during the week—like chameleons hidden from predators.

Certainly in some countries the consequences of being openly Christian can bring economic or even physical suffering. An Iranian man at our church who converted from Islam to follow Jesus showed me the medical report with accompanying photographs detailing his brutal physical tortures and lasting psychiatric damage when he was arrested for trying to evangelise his community.

In the West the opposition has, until recently, been generally subtle. Perhaps pitying parents have asked us to stop talking about Jesus; or scornful atheistic friends have unfriended us on Facebook because they're tired of our invitations to church; or work colleagues have expressed frustration with our morality, declaring us to be bigoted and dangerous.

But the opposition is getting more hostile in Western cultures. Our children can be humiliated at school for the biblical view of marriage we've taught them; university

Christian Unions find their speakers "cancelled" because they are considered homophobic by their Student Union; Christian doctors and teachers can find themselves facing a disciplinary process for offering to pray with a patient or student. Christian employees are refused their traditional carol service after complaints from humanists. Or perhaps we've been sent for "diversity training" for quietly expressing our reservations about championing Stonewall.

Trying to navigate between just causes such as racial equality in the aftermath of the appalling murder of George Floyd in Minneapolis in May 2020—and more dubious agendas such as gender fluidity—is fraught with problems for most of us. We're told that Christian morality is no longer the mainstream ethic of our society (despite most of our culture's principles of justice and equity having biblical origins). We find ourselves increasingly caught up in the bewildering efforts of governments, institutions, businesses and educators to comply with the demands of the tidal wave of causes ferociously competing for preferment on grounds of historic victimisation.

Any perceived divergence by us from swiftly evolving political correctness is met with vengeful rage on social media. It's hardly surprising that many Christians feel pressured to shrink back from public loyalty to Jesus and abandon all efforts to initiate evangelistic conversations— indeed, to behave increasingly like chameleons.

HEBREWS WAS WRITTEN FOR CHRISTIANS UNDER PRESSURE

The letter to the Hebrews was written for discouraged Jewish Christians, probably living in Rome, afflicted with the chameleon syndrome. They were not tempted to go back to Judaism. They were tempted to hide their faith.

We don't know who the author was. But he was clearly a deeply learned pastor who knew his Old Testament and loved his readers very much. Hebrews is his beautifully written extended sermon expounding a series of Old Testament texts. He calls his readers to keep listening to what God has spoken in the gospel of his Son, Jesus Christ. He combines dire warnings of judgment upon any who shrink back from Christ with warm encouragements of lasting heavenly blessing for all who remain loyal.

Eleven times in Hebrews he describes God's revelation in Jesus as "better" than anything in the Old Testament: a *better word* in the gospel than came from angels, Moses or Joshua (chapters 1 – 4); a *better priest* in heaven than in any temple on earth (chapters 5 – 7); a *better covenant* arrangement with God, based on forgiveness rather than on law we cannot keep (chapter 8), established by Jesus' *better sacrifice* as our true substitute on the cross, which animal sacrifices could never be (chapters 9 – 10). Jesus is *far better* than the best alternatives.

The author of Hebrews urgently pleads with his readers to "pay the most careful attention, therefore, to what we have heard" (2 v 1); "see to it, brothers and sisters, that none of you has a sinful, unbelieving heart that turns away from the living God. But encourage one another daily" (3 v 12-13); "let us draw near to God... let us hold unswervingly to the hope we profess ... let us consider how we may spur one another on ... not giving up meeting together, as some are in the habit of doing, but encouraging one another" (10 v 22-25) and now in our passage to "persevere" (10 v 36).

Hebrews calls weary Christians then and now to persevere and not shrink back, for which purpose the writer has penned one of the most powerfully encouraging passages in the whole Bible: the famous Hebrews 11.

Chapter 11 is a reminder from Old Testament history of how God has enabled his people down the centuries to endure by faith in him. It celebrates the faith of our Christian ancestors—our spiritual family. First from Genesis in the lives of the "ancients", it looks at Abel, Enoch and Noah; and then the great "patriarchs"— Abraham and Sarah, Isaac, Jacob and Joseph. Next the writer explores the faith-driven choices of Moses in Exodus, and then speeds up with Joshua, the judges and the prophets. The author aims to inspire his readers (including us) with these famous characters from Bible history whom he calls "such a great cloud of witnesses" (12 v 1) and who are cheering us on.

He's not suggesting that they're watching us from heaven. He's saying they encourage us from the pages of Scripture. And they're not a "great" cloud because they're so marvellous (many were not) but because there are so many of them.

Chapter 11 is sometimes unhelpfully described as "heroes of faith". Actually, they're not a select group of heroes at all. Indeed, it's hard to remember anyone in the Old Testament who's left out! The whole point is that God has *always* empowered persevering faith in his people. The author is demonstrating what God can enable all his readers to do by faith. He is showing what God can empower us to do.

So he doesn't just select the best people. Abraham and Moses certainly did make some remarkable decisions because of their faith. But there are plenty of others named who were very unimpressive, or even disgraceful, people. Instead of selecting heroic judges such as Othniel, Ehud and Deborah, he chooses famous disappointments like Gideon and Barak, who were utterly feeble, and Samson and Jephthah, who were depressingly shallow. The author is not describing the faith of an elite few. He's selecting some big moments when God enabled faith in the lives of very ordinary believers down the centuries— not to make heroes of them but to remind his readers of how God has enabled his people, including screw-ups like most of us, to persevere though all sorts of difficulty by faith. This chapter is not about superhuman faith. It's about the kind of faith God has always given his people from the very beginning.

To illustrate from the walls of many schools: Hebrews 11 is not an honours board for especially heroic champions. It's the wall covered with class photos from every year since the school began. Chapter 11 is not about heroes of faith. It's about God empowering ordinary people like us!

Which brings us to another vital observation. There are no chapter divisions in the original New Testament documents. The list in chapter 11 reaches its crescendo in Jesus, described in 12 v 1-3. The author uses rhetorical skills such as quickening the repetition of the phrase "by faith" and adding lists of examples without conjunctions to build the excitement of the passage towards Jesus. For the whole message of Hebrews is that Jesus is *better* than all. Jesus is our *Hero of faith*. Everything that faith enabled the people of chapter 11 to do finds its *perfection* in Jesus. The author has told his readers in 10 v 36 that "you need to persevere", so his climactic description of Jesus reads, "And let us run with perseverance the race marked out for us, fixing our eyes on Jesus, the pioneer and perfecter of faith" (12 v 1-2). He's calling them supremely to fix their eyes not on the flawed characters of chapter 11 but on Jesus, whose endurance of the cross is the champion example of living by faith.

INTRODUCING THE HEBREWS

The passage immediately before chapter 11 helps clarify the situation of the Hebrew readers to whom chapter 11 was written, which is so important for understanding what the author means and for drawing appropriate applications. They have previously endured costly persecution:

> Remember those earlier days after you had received the light [of gospel truth], when you *endured* in a great conflict full of suffering. Sometimes you were publicly exposed to insult and persecution; at other

times you stood side by side with those who were so
treated.   (Hebrews 10 v 32-33)

Many of the readers were veteran believers who had
courageously maintained public loyalty to Christ through
a "great conflict" (v 32) or struggle: probably the expulsion
of Jews from Rome by Emperor Claudius in AD 49 because
of rioting about *Chrestus*, presumably Jesus Christ. Being
"exposed to insult" means suffering public humiliation,
and "persecution" implies physical suffering for Jesus—
though not yet to the point of shedding blood (12 v 4, as
many Christian were later cruelly killed in Roman arenas
for entertainment). Imagine the physical and emotional
trauma involved, especially for the children.

When they'd first experienced the joy of forgiveness
in Christ, they'd been zealous for the gospel. But their
enthusiasm was draining way. For it isn't only new
believers who are tempted to hide; experienced Christians
grow weary and feel discouraged too. Perhaps some of
us are respected in our church because of our zeal in the
past. But in truth we haven't commended Jesus or invited
anyone to church for a long while, let alone brought
anyone to Christ. Perhaps we can remember how we were
once urgent in prayer for world mission, listening to God
in his word every day, making radical sacrifices of time
and money for our church—but not for some years now.

I'm an experienced church pastor now, and I know this
temptation to rely on past exploits is very real for church
leaders too. But living by faith is not living in the past. It
means *living by faith today*—not winding down to wither
away but stepping up to make our later years the most

productive ones for the gospel. Like in the conversation I've just had with a man from our church who's been able to retire early—not to play golf and bridge but to do some theological training to invest more time in his prison ministry and serve in one of our missional community groups. Hebrews 11 will be vital for mature believers tempted to *retire* from living by faith just as much as for younger believers tempted to *fear* living by faith.

In the past, these Hebrews had joyfully accepted the loss of their property because of their confidence in heaven:

> You suffered along with those in prison and joyfully accepted the confiscation of your property, because you knew that you yourselves had better and lasting possessions [in the new creation of heaven].
>
> (Hebrews 10 v 34)

They'd previously sympathised with believers in prison and without self-pity had joyfully "accepted" (literally "welcomed") the seizure of their property—presumably from looting or eviction. Imagine them sitting in their ransacked homes after the violent mob has left, gathering terrified family members together to thank God in prayer for the privilege of suffering for Jesus. How could they "welcome" such a cost? Because they were looking forward to their glorious inheritance in heaven!

Jesus said in his Sermon on the Mount:

> Blessed are those who are persecuted because of righteousness,
>   for theirs is the kingdom of heaven.

Blessed are you when people insult you, persecute you and falsely say all kinds of evil against you because of me. Rejoice and be glad, because great is your reward in heaven.   (Matthew 5 v 10-12)

Do not store up for yourselves treasures on earth ... but store up for yourselves treasures in heaven.
(Matthew 6 v 19-20)

We need to remember this the next time the church treasurer asks for funding for gospel mission.

But now these readers were flagging: tempted to "drift away" from the gospel (2 v 1), "turn away" from God (3 v 12), harden their hearts in "disobedience" to God's word (4 v 11), become "lazy" (6 v 12), and "throw away" their confidence in the gospel promise (10 v 35). So the author says:

So do not throw away your confidence; it will be richly rewarded. You need to *persevere* so that when you have done the will of God, you will receive what he has promised. For, "In just a little while, he who is coming will come and not delay." And, "But my righteous one will *live by faith*. And I take no pleasure in the one who shrinks back."
(Hebrews 10 v 35-38)

They have to persevere in obeying God's will published in Scripture if they want to receive the glorious joy in heaven that is promised by the gospel. The author speaks plainly with the authority of two Old Testament quotes. First, Isaiah 26 says God will certainly come in judgment—there will be no delay or change of plan. Then in Habakkuk 2, when Habakkuk was upset with God for using Babylonian armies to punish Israel, God told Habakkuk to wait patiently, *living by faith* in God's promises. For God will not be pleased with anyone who "shrinks back" from living by faith (Hebrews 10 v 38)! Hebrews 11 is an illustrated exposition of this quote.

The writer is telling his readers that they must persevere! There is no alternative. When Christ returns, no one will survive his judgment with tales from the distant past—like dining out on exaggerated stories of winning the under-tens race at school. Being a Christian is like running a marathon, and Christ will only be pleased with those who keep running: not shrinking back from openly living by faith, whatever the cost—ragged and exhausted maybe, but persevering to the end! So the author is writing to say...

YOU CAN DO THIS!

He remains utterly confident that they can endure in their saving faith because God has always empowered his people to keep going *by faith*, as the author is about to illustrate in chapter 11:

> But we do not belong to those who shrink back and are destroyed, but to those who have faith and are saved.   (Hebrews 10 v 39)

Christians are tempted to shrink back from public loyalty to Christ when we forget where we belong. We don't belong to this godless world that we so foolishly try to impress.

And we don't belong with fairweather church people who drift away when they feel the scorching heat of criticism—which reveals that they were never truly God's people, for "when trouble or persecution comes because of the word, they quickly fall away" (Mark 4 v 17).

We belong with the great cloud of witnesses in chapter 11, who didn't shrink back, and with our church family who are not shrinking back either. That's why we need to read our Bibles (to hear from past generations of our family) and go to church each week (to hear from our present spiritual family), and be reminded where we belong—with "those who have faith and are saved".

The Covid-19 lockdown has reminded us of how much we need to be with our church family physically and not just online. And if you are someone who has previously been slack in attending church, allowing weekend breaks or family commitments or sporting fixtures to restrict your church and small-group attendance, perhaps you need to recognise where you belong and resolve to be regularly at church. Remember the simple illustration of coals on a fire: take a coal off the fire and it goes cold, but put it back on the fire and it becomes hot again. If you are a Christian, you don't belong with those who shrink back, who are facing everlasting destruction. You belong with those who are saved and living by faith. You need the encouragement of your church to live by faith—and your church family needs your encouragement too!

For the faith the author is about to *describe* in 11 v 1-2 and *illustrate* in 11 v 3-40 is not an optional extra. If we shrink back from this faith, we will not be saved.

For saving faith is not just *active* (as James teaches) but *persevering* (as Hebrews teaches).

It's not that we save ourselves by persevering, nor that we're saved initially by God's grace, and then have to keep going ourselves. No, our salvation is entirely by God's grace—but by him empowering our enduring faith in the gospel of Christ. God empowers our persevering faith *through our daily relationship with Christ*, the author and perfecter of persevering faith. So this faith is not only what God *requires* but what God *provides*!

That's why the author challenges his readers in verse 36: "You need to persevere" if you want to be saved; and then reassures them in verse 39: "We do not belong to those who shrink back and are destroyed". He knows God will use his challenge to enable the Hebrew readers to *persevere*, in order to *preserve* them in saving faith.

BE LIKE LAKE GALILEE

There are three very different lakes in Palestine connected by the Jordan River. Lake Galilee is the middle of the three. To the north of Lake Galilee, Lake Huleh is usually dry as dust because it has no substantial tributary running into it and any rainfall runs straight south to Lake Galilee. However, south of Lake Galilee is the Dead Sea, so named because it has no outflow and is therefore full of poisonous salts, and nothing lives in it. But Lake Galilee lies between Lake Huleh and the Dead Sea, with both a tributary bringing in fresh water and an outlet washing out the salts, so that it's full of life and supports a vibrant fishing industry.

In different seasons of life, Christians are like each of these lakes. Some of us are too much like the Dead Sea: we've enjoyed plenty of input in sound Bible-teaching but have done little with it to build others up and have become poisonous—like "expository police" with a critical spirit venting on social media and causing division and discouragement. We need to find some gospel outreach to serve in.

But most of us are more like Lake Huleh, spiritually dry as dust. We've been giving out in costly service for so long that we're spiritually exhausted and drained dry— like the Hebrews. We need to be more like Lake Galilee with fresh spiritual encouragement from Scripture as well as opportunities to serve in our local church. Then we'll be spiritually fresh with a thriving evangelistic fishing ministry.

If you are feeling the pressure to hide like a chameleon, if you fear the cost of open loyalty to Jesus and are tempted to "shrink back": then Hebrews 11 is for you. It's the spiritual refreshment we need to persevere, "by faith".

1. CONFIDENT

Faith is confidence in God's word

Now faith is confidence in what we hope for and
assurance about what we do not see. This is what the
ancients were commended for. By faith we understand
that the universe was formed at God's command, so that
what is seen was not made out of what was visible.

(Hebrews 11 v 1-3)

God has always empowered his people to endure by faith and not shrink back. This is not just people from the distant past. You may have heard of the courageous Nigerian schoolgirl, Leah Sharibu, the only Christian among 110 girls abducted in February 2018 by the violent extremist Muslim group, Boko Haram, in north-east Nigeria. All the girls were released a month later except Leah because she refused to renounce Christ and convert to Islam. She was 17. Now she and a Christian nurse have been told they will be enslaved for life and at the mercy of violent terrorists. How could Leah be so resolute? The answer is, by faith: the same faith that God creates and strengthens in all his people through his word. I'm not claiming we will never shrink back or will always be loyal to Jesus. I'm saying we can be, by faith.

I've told the story many times of arriving in Sydney to begin some theological study at Moore College, when the principal kindly collected me from the airport and took me back to his house for dinner with his family. After the meal, as we washed up, he asked me a penetrating question: "What one word do you think best summarises the Christian life?" I panicked. I had no idea what to say. I tried sounding pious and said, "Holiness?" but he was clearly unconvinced. So I tried sounding humble and said, "Sin?" and he looked horrified! Eventually, he finally put me out of my misery and suggested, "How about *faith*?"

The reason I'm repeating this story is that he was saying something huge. Some offer a version of the Christian life that they claim will bring success; others offer a life which is all about morality; others still offer a life lost in mystery. But the Bible offers a Christian life characterised by *faith* (also translated "believing") in God's word of gospel promise. So, when Jesus went into Galilee to begin proclaiming "the word", he declared, "The kingdom of God has come near. Repent and believe [i.e. live by faith in] the good news!" (Mark 1 v 15) And Paul writes, "For it is by grace you have been saved, through faith—and this is not from yourselves, it is the gift of God" (Ephesians 2 v 8).

But what is this faith through which God saves people? In Western thinking, Christian faith is commonly regarded at best as groundless optimism and at worst as ignorant, irrational and dangerous fantasy. Secular atheist Christopher Hitchens, author of *God Is Not Great: Why Religion Poisons Everything*, once declared, "Faith is the surrender of the mind; it's the surrender of reason, it's the surrender of the only thing that makes us different from other mammals" (*The Telegraph*, 13th April 2011). Indeed it is common for Christians to be regarded as unscientific and anti-intellectual (though in truth, when people become Christians, they characteristically think and read more than ever before). Hebrews 11 will powerfully refute this misconception of Christian faith.

Interestingly, the search engine Google offers two definitions of faith: "Complete trust or confidence in someone or something" and then "Belief in the doctrines of a religion, based on spiritual conviction rather than proof". While many religions may be fairly described as the second, Christian faith is the first. Christian faith is relational trust and confidence in God, based upon rational evidence of his truthful reliability. Christian faith is not irrational fantasy or sentimental optimism. It is confidence in the truth revealed by God in his *personal word*, Jesus Christ—as he is revealed in his *written word*, the Bible. Being true, the Bible is consistent with natural truth discovered by scientists. So while Christian faith is certainly more than scientific, it is not less than scientific.

We could just say that faith is personal trust in Jesus. But there are so many versions of Jesus that we have to clarify: we believe in the Jesus revealed in God's gospel as this is explained in the Bible. The New Testament defines

God's gospel in various places (e.g. Romans 1 v 1-4) as the good news (not good advice or good ideas) that Jesus is Christ our Lord—who came as our King, died for our sins, rose to rule and will return to judge (Mark 1 v 14; 1 Corinthians 15 v 1-7; Romans 2 v 16). And through faith in this gospel, we enjoy a new life of peace, hope and righteousness as citizens of God's heavenly kingdom as we wait for Christ's return to judge and renew his creation. The gospel is God's promise of heaven. Christian faith is trusting his gospel promise.

People sometimes excuse themselves from considering faith in Christ by saying, "I just don't have your faith"— but they do. Everyone has faith. We exercise faith when we sit on a chair trusting it not to collapse, or open our mouth trusting a dentist to rearrange our teeth, or get on a bus trusting the driver to take us home. Everyone has faith. What makes a Christian distinctive is not our faith but where our faith is placed—namely, in God's gospel promise of heaven through Jesus Christ. The ability to have faith, to trust and believe, is given by God to all humanity. But all human beings sinfully and stubbornly refuse to trust in God. So, faith in Christ must be given by God. It is given by God only to those to whom God has chosen to give it. And it is given by his Holy Spirit through his gospel word.

Some believers worry that their faith is too simple or that it will never become as strong as that of others. We certainly don't need a complicated faith to be saved. Jesus said that faith as small as a mustard seed (which is tiny) is effective (Matthew 17 v 20), if it is placed in the Jesus of the gospel. And he taught that at the heart of everyone's saving faith there must be a child-like trust in God (Matthew 18 v 2). This doesn't mean our faith must stay *childish* in depth but *child-like* in trust. And since "faith comes from hearing the message" (Romans 10 v 17), our faith will grow stronger the more we understand God's word. That's why we need to read our Bibles, only listen to careful Bible-teaching online, and, above all, look to attend a church where we will hear God's word being carefully explained.

FAITH IS CONFIDENCE IN GOD'S WORD ABOUT FUTURE AND UNSEEN REALTIES

The writer to the Hebrews wants to encourage and challenge his readers to persevere by explaining and illustrating two aspects of what such saving faith can do, which reappear throughout chapter 11.

In verse 1 he explains, "Now faith is confidence in what we hope for and assurance about what we do not see."

This certainly isn't a full definition of saving faith. It doesn't explain how faith in Christ is paired with repentance from sin in turning to God for salvation (Acts 20 v 21); nor how faith derives from the hope offered in the gospel promise and is expressed in dependent prayer and obedient love (Colossians 1; Galatians 5). It doesn't explain the place of faith in the sequence of God's salvation (the *ordo salutis*)—that by his sovereign grace God has foreknown, elected and predestined many from among sinners to be ransomed by Jesus on the cross and then called by his Spirit through the gospel to new life ("reborn" or "regenerated"), which is expressed in faith—by which we are incorporated into Christ and so justified (counted "righteous" and acceptable in Christ) and thereafter sanctified and preserved for glory in heaven with Jesus—to the eternal praise of God! (If that last bit frazzled your brain, don't worry; it's taken the best theologians two thousand years to work that out.)

But this famous description in Hebrews 11 v 1 concentrates upon the two parallel aspects of faith that enable Christians to persevere through opposition and struggle:

> Now faith is confidence in what we hope for
> and assurance about what we do not see.

The word translated as "confidence" (*hypostasis*) means a solid guarantee. "What we hope for" is the future promised by God's gospel: namely our inheritance in heaven—the overwhelming pleasure of enjoying God in his spectacular glory. At the end of the Bible we're given stunning images of life in heaven with Jesus as a spectacular wedding feast—a vast multicultural festival for believers from all nations, with the river of the water of life, clear as crystal, satisfying the spiritual thirst of our souls, the tree of life symbolising the cross of Christ sustaining and healing the damage of sin in our characters for ever (Revelation 7; 22).

I was privileged to be with my children in the London 2012 Olympic stadium on "Super Saturday" when British athletes Greg Rutherford, Jessica Ennis and Mo Farah all won gold in 46 insanely exciting minutes. I've never experienced anything like it. The crowd of 80,000 was absolutely jumping. But from the Bible's incredible descriptions of being in heaven celebrating Jesus' triumphs, that night in London will seem like watching paint dry in a library! So first, *Christian faith is firm confidence in the future promised by God in heaven.*

Perhaps this matters most to those of us who are grieving for a loved one who has died in Christ.

The word translated as "assurance" (*elenchos*) means active certainty. "What we do not see" means spiritual realities that are absolutely real but invisible, including God himself. So Christian faith is not like a *Star Wars* film, *imagining* a planet called Tatooine from where Luke Skywalker comes. Christian faith is like the NASA James Webb Space Telescope, the most powerful telescope ever built, able to *see* distant galaxies from far away. Faith enables us to see realities that are invisible but do exist.

So second, *Christian faith is resolute confidence in the unseen spiritual realities of God.*

Put together, Christian faith is solid confidence in future and unseen realities promised in God's word.

Notice that although these future and unseen realities are not accessible to our physical senses, they are still real. I used to think that faith helps us believe God's word *without* experience. But that needs to be nuanced because faith *is* experiential. Faith grants us some experience of realities that unbelievers simply cannot perceive, although the full experience of them awaits us in the new creation. So when the apostle Paul says, "We live by faith, not by sight" (2 Corinthians 5 v 7), he is not saying that we live without any sensible or experiential basis for what we believe. He is saying that we live by what we know of future and unseen realities revealed to us in God's utterly reliable word, the Bible. So faith is confidence in things promised in the gospel that are either "what we hope for" (the future new creation) or "what we do not see" (the spiritual realms).

This isn't a complete definition of faith. But it's what flagging Christians need. We are like weary runners, who need to be able to see the finishing line ahead. God gives Christians faith to see the future and the unseen realities that he has promised us in his word. His Holy Spirit enables us to see them in black and white on the pages of our Bibles.

"This," says the writer to the Hebrews, "is what the ancients were commended for"—by God in the Bible, as the writer is about to illustrate. What God delights to find in his people of every age and culture is confidence in his word. He takes no delight in imaginary "pie-in-the-sky-when-you-die" fantasies. He delights in such confidence because relational trust is beautiful; it honours faithfulness in the person trusted. When a husband says to his wife before she gives a terrifying public address, "You can do this. I believe in you", he is reassuring her of his confidence in her powers of public speaking. When a wife tells her husband travelling abroad on a business trip, "I trust you", she is reassuring him of her confidence in his character. When we tell God, "I trust you; I believe in you; I have faith in your gospel", we are telling him that we have confidence in his power and his character. So faith is worship!

WE BELIEVE IN CREATION, THOUGH WE WEREN'T THERE TO SEE IT

The writer now launches into his list of examples of what God has always enabled his people to do by faith. His first is the basic conviction of every Christian that God created the universe, which requires faith in the very first verse of the Bible:

> By faith we understand that the universe was formed at God's command, so that what is seen was not made out of what was visible. (Hebrews 11 v 3)

The universe is obviously amazing. From the ever-changing information available online, it seems that astronomers reckon from data gained from the Hubble and Hipparcos satellites that our *observable* universe is 93 billion light years wide. Mathematicians therefore reckon that there are at least 2 trillion galaxies averaging 100 million stars each in our universe, adding up to a mind-boggling 10 billion billion stars like our sun with all their planets and moons (Wikipedia: "Galaxy"). Genesis 1 tells us, "In the beginning God created the heavens and the earth" (v 1). So—perhaps by using whatever big bang and evolutionary processes scientists are now discovering—God made everything out of nothing by the power of his word; and with a passing comment the writer of Genesis observes, "He also made the stars" (v 16). He has decorated the night sky with jewels to display his glory and call us to worship him.

The search goes on among scientists for the "theory of everything", which is also the title of the 2014 film starring Eddie Redmayne about the life of legendary theoretical physicist Stephen Hawking, who died in 2018. Apparently, the "theory of everything" refers to the search for an all-encompassing theory that can accommodate the general theory of relativity with quantum physics and string theory in one uniting truth. While cosmologists (including many Christians) search for *how* this might work, the Bible has already told us the *who* and the *why* of creation: God created the universe out of nothing as the dwelling for people who are to be saved by the self-sacrifice of his Son to enjoy and glorify him in heaven for ever. We know this, although we weren't there to see it happen, by faith in Genesis 1, which proclaims, "In the beginning God created the heavens and the earth" by his word out of nothing, and tells us that it was "very good".

Christians believe this, but not because our faith is a stupid, blind leap in the dark whereby we must remain ignorant of science. God's "book of Creation" (the natural world), properly interpreted by scientists, and his "book of Christ" (the Bible), properly interpreted by preachers, reinforce each other. So Christian faith does not need to avoid science. Indeed, many of the world's greatest scientists have been and are Christians. It's important to explore this relationship between the Bible and science a little further, so that we don't imagine we have to defend a kind of blind faith that ignores what is obvious from science.

GOOD SCIENCE SUGGESTS GOD – AS THUNDER SUGGESTS LIGHTNING

Scientists cannot see from nature *why* anything exists. But scientific observation has uncovered many realities logically pointing to the biblical revelation of God, just as hearing thunder logically points to lightning even if we didn't see the lightning flash. If we compare God to lightning, here are *six peals of thunder*—echoes of God in our experience of the natural world—that point the open-minded to the existence of a divine Creator.

a) Our existence

Scientists know of nothing in the cosmos that exists without a cause; logically this suggests something or someone supernatural as the first cause to trigger the "big bang" (namely, God).

b) Our precarious design

Scientists are amazed by the perfectly tuned balances of nature that enable human life, such as between the speed of light, nuclear forces and gravity, so that humanity is like a ping-pong ball suspended by jets of air in the middle of a room. To insist that we're here by accident is like insisting that jumbo jets come from tornados blowing through garages! And suggesting that we're accidentally one of an infinite number of alternatives in a multiverse still requires someone to have chosen from the alternatives (i.e. God). Something so precariously designed for human life as our world in this universe most logically suggests a designer. It is said that the great

Christian physicist Isaac Newton was once visited by an atheist colleague who, seeing Newton's complex model of the solar system in his front room exclaimed, "Isaac, what a wonderful model you've made!" Newton cheekily replied, "Oh, no one made it. It happened by accident!"

Our precarious and complex existence reverberates loudly with evidence of a creative designer (namely, God).

c) Our instinctive morality

Most of us regard the savagery of genocide or the injustice of racism as evil; but if there's no God authorising such instinctive morality, then slaughter and prejudice are just examples of genetic competition and evolutionary selection. As atheist Richard Dawkins puts it, "In a universe of ... blind physical forces and genetic replication, some people are going to get hurt, other people are going to get lucky, and you won't find any rhyme or reason in it, nor any justice" (*River Out of Eden: A Darwinian View of Life, p133*). The more sensible explanation for our instinctive moral desire to protect the weak, confer human rights and encourage social charity is that we are shaped by a moral being beyond our selfish genes (our own instinctive morality is another echo of God).

d) Our self-awareness

Atheists struggle adequately to explain any benefit to our survival in our human capacity for self-aware thinking or abstract philosophy, to reflect on the past or to imagine a future, let alone our irrepressible religious instincts, which are all unnecessary for survival (these are another echo of God).

e) Our delight in beauty

If our appreciation of appearance derives subconsciously merely from acquiring a good breeding partner or sustainable sources of food, then why do we gratuitously delight in beauty, even when it inhibits our breeding or survival? Delight in beauty doesn't help us breed (romance fuels commitment, which limits copulation). If there's no God and we're just living in a material world, why are we inspired by Tennyson's poem about the suicidal charge of the Light Brigade or by a Mumford and Sons lament to wait for a lover? And why on earth do we find people lovely when they're old or disabled? Our irrepressible delight in beauty that has nothing to do with reproduction is a thunderous echo of God!

f) Our emotional longings

If there's no God, then why do we experience powerful yearnings to contribute something to the common good, for satisfaction in our work, for freedom from guilt in our souls, to be free in ways that don't hurt other people, to be precious without diminishing others, for justice in a credible moral framework—and for life beyond the grave! We have so many deep, transcendent longings that are nothing to do with genetic replication: peals of thunder proclaiming that lightning exists. Science discovers what Psalm 19 declares: "The heavens declare the glory of God"—he is invisible but real. Faith that believes that

God created the world is not unscientific or irrational but logically consistent with the best science.

IF GOD CREATED THIS WORLD, HE CAN KEEP HIS PROMISE TO DO IT AGAIN

But in every age and culture, human beings have sinfully tried to "suppress the truth" about God proclaimed by nature, "for since the creation of the world God's invisible qualities—his eternal power and divine nature—have been clearly seen, being understood from what has been made, so that people are without excuse. For although they knew God, they neither glorified him as God nor gave thanks to him, but their thinking became futile and their foolish hearts were darkened" (Romans 1 v 18, 20-21).

So why do Christians all believe, contrary to the prevailing scepticism of our culture, that God created the universe out of nothing, when none of us were there to see it? "By faith we understand that the universe was formed at God's command" because Genesis 1 says, "In the beginning God created the heavens and the earth", and he did it by his Spirit though his word (Psalm 33 v 6).

The writer is showing his weary Hebrew readers that if they still believe God created the universe out of nothing by his word, they can also trust his gospel promise of a new creation for his recreated people one day. For we actually live in the evidence for the power of his word: in a world that didn't exist until God commanded it into existence. If God has promised to resurrect us into a new creation, we can believe him because we know he's done it before. And every amazing new TV documentary series celebrating the natural world, like *Blue Planet*, *Frozen Planet* or *Our Planet*, serves to remind us of the power of God to keep his gospel promise of a new creation in heaven.

How can we shrink back from loyalty to Christ when every night sky and every rumble of thunder reminds us of his power to keep his promises? God's word has promised us "an inheritance that can never perish, spoil or fade ... kept in heaven for you" even though for now we may have to suffer all kinds of trials (1 Peter 1 v 4, 6). We can trust that promise even if everyone in the office tells us it's nonsense, because, by faith in his word, we know what God can do.

You too can be confident—sure of what you hope for (confident in God's power to keep his promise of a new creation) and certain of what you do not see (confident in God's loving provision even though you can't see him)— because you live in an amazing universe that proves the power of God's word!

2. COMMENDED

By faith the ancients were commended by God

By faith Abel brought God a better offering than Cain did. By faith he was commended as righteous, when God spoke well of his offerings. And by faith Abel still speaks, even though he is dead.

By faith Enoch was taken from this life, so that he did not experience death: "He could not be found, because God had taken him away." For before he was taken, he was commended as one who pleased God. And without faith it is impossible to please God, because anyone who comes to him must believe that he exists and that he rewards those who earnestly seek him.

By faith Noah, when warned about things not yet seen, in holy fear built an ark to save his family. By his faith he condemned the world and became heir of the righteousness that is in keeping with faith.

(Hebrews 11 v 4-7)

My favourite movies are all historical dramas: *Darkest Hour, Titanic, Hidden Figures, Schindler's List, The King's Speech, Black Hawk Down, Amadeus, Fury, Frost/ Nixon* and so on. History is so much more interesting when it's not just dates and facts but presented as a human story. And films are so much more inspiring when you know they're based on real people. (I love it when they show you photos at the end.) Please don't despair—I do love *Notting Hill* and *Warrior*, but make-believe just isn't as inspiring as real life.

That's what Hebrews 11 gives us: short, captivating historical dramas. They're punchy and varied. (Some characters like Abraham and Moses are well known, but who's ever heard of Enoch and Jephthah?) And they're inspiring, especially when we read the background accounts in the Old Testament.

Having described faith as confidence in future and unseen spiritual realities promised by God in his word (v 1-3), the author now presents an amazing series of historical vignettes to show what God enables his people to do by faith. He has recommended this approach before:

> We do not want you to become lazy, but to imitate
> those who through faith and patience inherit what
> has been promised. (Hebrews 6 v 12)

He knows that Christians benefit enormously from reading encouraging biographies, especially those God provides for us in his word. Each of the illustrations in Hebrews 11 is crafted to build up a composite picture of faith, (like assembling the pieces of a jigsaw), which is completed by the crescendo in Jesus (12 v 1-3).

The first three examples, "the ancients", share in the fundamental blessing of having their faith "commended" by God (v 2). Being commended or approved by God is actually our greatest human need. But this approval is not something superficial, like a round of applause or a "like" on Facebook. This word "commended" conveys the idea of a conclusive legal defence in court. If God testifies that we are acceptable to him, then our access to the blessings of his presence are secured for ever. Indeed, when we know we're accepted and cherished by God, we can endure the rejection and scorn of unbelievers instead of desperately chasing their approval.

Reaching back to the beginning of our salvation history, after the rebellion of our original ancestors, Adam and Eve, we begin with Abel, the first believer.

BY FAITH ABEL OFFERED A BLOOD SACRIFICE AND WAS COMMENDED BY GOD

By faith Abel brought God a better offering than Cain did. By faith he was commended as righteous, when God spoke well of his offerings. And by faith Abel still speaks, even though he is dead.

(Hebrews 11 v 4)

There is a fuller account of these brothers in Genesis 4. There we read that Cain grew up to farm crops while Abel kept flocks. Both brothers brought sacrifices to God, expressing their awareness of needing God's approval combined with the consciousness that we are not acceptable in ourselves. So they brought offerings.

However hard we try to believe the secular spin that we're totally lovely as we are and accountable to no one but ourselves, all but the most arrogant of us are aware to some degree of our failings. That's why we make such costly sacrifices in our attempts to impress: perhaps dieting and exercising furiously or spending a fortune on clothes to look great; or maybe working all hours to acquire wealth and status that will earn the respect of our family or colleagues; or maybe we're rushing around madly trying to please everybody!

Many people bring the same approach into their relationship with God—such sacrificial effort to gain approval is at the heart of all major religions. That's what seems at first sight to be happening here; both Cain and Abel brought sacrifices. Genesis tells us that Cain brought some of "the fruits of the soil", from his harvest; Abel brought "fat portions from some of the firstborn of his flock". This sounds as if they each brought something costly from their different lives.

When we read in Genesis 4 that "the LORD looked with favour on Abel and his offering, but on Cain and his offering he did not look with favour", it sounds arbitrary and unfair. So we're not surprised when verse 5 tells us that "Cain was very angry, and his face was downcast". It seems surprising when the Lord confronts Cain to warn him: "Sin is crouching at your door; it desires to have you, but you must rule over it". Tragically, Cain invites Abel into the fields where, in his jealous rage, he murders his brother.

It's a shocking crime.

Obviously, we can't approve of Cain's overreaction, but why would God approve of Abel's offering and not Cain's? Why do we read here in Hebrews "By faith Abel brought God a better offering than Cain did. By faith he was commended as righteous, when God spoke well of his offerings"?

Notice three crucial details.

a) God was pleased by the *faith* that motivated Abel

Cain offered a sacrifice—as religious people do—trying to impress God and earn his approval. But Abel's sacrifice was motivated by the faith within his heart. The author of Hebrews would have known the prophet Isaiah's condemnation of faithless sacrifices—"Their hearts are far from me" (Isaiah 29 v 13)—and he is about to explain that "without faith it is impossible to please God" (Hebrews 11 v 6). So although Genesis 4 doesn't mention Abel's faith, the writer of Hebrews knows that God would only approve of Abel's sacrifice if it came from Abel's personal faith in God. That's why verse 4 doesn't just say, "By faith Abel brought a better offering" but "By faith Abel brought *God* a better offering". Abel wasn't just making a costly religious sacrifice to *bribe* God, as religious people do. He was making a sacrifice to *please* God as part of his personal faith in the living God, whom he worshipped.

Like Abel, let us also ensure that our sacrifices of money, time and effort in church are not merely religious bribes but motivated by a personal and loving faith in God.

b) God was pleased by Abel's faith expressed in bringing a blood sacrifice

The text calls this a "better sacrifice". (Hebrews repeatedly commends what is "better".) It's not just the commercial value of the "fat portions from some of the firstborn of the flock" which Abel brought that was better. This offering involved the death of an animal, pointing forward initially to the Passover and Day of Atonement sacrifices in the temple, but ultimately to the bloody death of the suffering servant, Jesus, on the cross to pay for our sins in our place. It's unlikely that Abel understood much of this, though he would have known that God had sacrificed an animal to provide skin clothing to cover the shame of his parents, Adam and Eve. Perhaps he'd begun to realise that his sin deserved death and so God's approval would only be possible through the death of a substitute.

Whatever he understood, the lesson for us is clear. Let's not imagine that we can impress God or secure his eternal approval with the fruit of our own lives. We will need the blood of Christ on the cross to satisfy God.

c) God commended Abel as "righteous"

Indeed, Jesus calls him, "righteous Abel" (Matthew 23 v 35). It's not that Abel accidentally stumbled across the right sacrifice to secure God's arbitrary approval. Rather, God graciously gives some sinners faith to trust his gospel promise: to realise that we have nothing to commend ourselves to God and so another must die in our place. And when we put this faith in God, he extravagantly reckons to us the perfect life of Christ to qualify us for heaven. When Abel demonstrated his faith, like every believer after him, God "commended him as righteous", declaring him "justified" in advance of judgment day, and qualified for access to God for ever.

When the Lord looked on Abel with favour, Cain hated his brother so much that he killed him. Cain could have been glad for his brother and asked Abel for advice. But those who want to impress God with their own good works (the essence of religion) will often see life as a moral competition (in which they intend to be winners) and feel angry with those who claim to be qualified by God's gift through faith (Christians) because salvation by faith diminishes the works they feel so proud of. Religious people like Cain will often find people like Abel annoying, and sometimes persecute them. The apostle John writes:

> Do not be like Cain, who belonged to the evil one
> and murdered his brother. And why did he murder
> him? Because his own actions were evil and his
> brother's were righteous. Do not be surprised, my
> brothers and sisters, if the world hates you.
>
> (1 John 3 v 12-13)

Don't be surprised when religious people, even some who are regular churchgoers, seem strangely hostile towards your faith in Christ. This is the spirit of Cain— the religious competitor hating those who are joyfully confident in Christ by faith.

When the author of Hebrews writes, "And by faith Abel still speaks, even though he is dead" (11 v 4), he means that the faith of Abel is still speaking to us now in the

Bible. This is a deliberate echo of God's confrontation with Cain: "Your brother's blood cries out to me from the ground" (Genesis 4 v 10). It was crying out for vengeance under the Law of Moses. But in Hebrews 12 we read that when we come to Jesus, we come to the "sprinkled blood that speaks a better word than the blood of Abel" (v 24). This is saying that while the blood of Abel called for the justice of God's vengeance in Genesis 4, the blood of Jesus now offers everyone, even hostile religious people, God's forgiveness and justification.

The simple encouragement for the Hebrews and for us is that Abel's faith promises commendation and acceptance from God for all who rely, by faith, on the blood sacrifice of Christ and not on our own religious bribes, as Cain did. We don't have to keep making sacrifices to try and impress God. We just need to rely by faith upon Christ's death for our sin on the cross. What a relief that is! If you put your faith in the death of Jesus instead of thinking you will impress him yourself, you can experience this joy too.

The next example of saving faith is even less well known than Abel...

BY FAITH ENOCH WALKED WITH GOD AND WAS COMMENDED BY GOD

By faith Enoch was taken from this life, so that he did not experience death: "He could not be found, because God had taken him away." For before he was taken, he was commended as one who pleased God. And without faith it is impossible to please God,

because anyone who comes to him must believe that
he exists and that he rewards those who earnestly
seek him.   (Hebrews 11 v 5-6)

In the intriguing example of Enoch, the writer doesn't
even tell us what Enoch did by his faith—almost certainly
because it was so easy to remember. Of the very little we
know about Enoch, twice in Genesis 5 it says that "Enoch
walked faithfully with God" (5 v 22, 24), followed by "then
he was no more, because God took him away". The author
of Hebrews 11 clearly wants his readers to reflect on
how faith enables us to "walk with God" because he then
writes, "For before he was taken, he was commended as
one who pleased God". As with Abel, he is again speaking
about how faith pleases God—that God will commend
the faith of Enoch in us, counting us righteous in Christ.
But if the faith of Abel is recognising our need of a blood
sacrifice to satisfy God, what is this faith of Enoch, who
"walked with God"?

It's important to remember what has previously
happened in Genesis 3. After their catastrophic rebellion
in the Garden of Eden, Adam and Eve "heard the sound
of the LORD God as he was walking in the garden in the
cool of the day [the evening]". Is that not amazing? The
biblical idea of "walking" with someone is the idea of
intimate friendship and fellowship. The living Lord God,
Creator of the universe, granted his people the privilege of
walking with him in paradise to talk intimately together!
What a joy—to hear the wisdom of the one who designed
creation and wrote the play in which we are playing a
small part, called history (his-story)!

But having rebelled by doubting and disobeying God's word, Adam and Eve were rightly afraid of God and hid from him (soon to be cast out into the wilderness to die far away from God). Yet by his faith, Enoch chose to be different and walked with God—and indeed is still walking with God in heaven! Enoch didn't just want to know *about* God; he wanted to walk *with* God! That's what Christian faith is: we don't just want to know about God; we want intimate fellowship with him, to walk with him and delight in him.

We don't know the details of how Enoch obtained this privilege. But our author observes, "And without faith it is impossible to please God, because anyone who comes to him must believe that he exists and that he rewards those who earnestly seek him" (Hebrews 11 v 6). Enoch believed in the *reality* of God (he exists) and the *generosity* of God (he rewards those who earnestly seek him). It's not hard to realise that God exists—the glory of creation testifies to it, as we have seen. Although atheistic philosophers and governments have tried to extinguish theism, they have failed to do so. Even in secular Britain, where we are regularly told that Christianity is finished, the British Social Attitudes Survey of 2018 revealed that while the proportion of people describing themselves as Christians has dropped to 38%, the proportion of people willing to say, "I don't believe in God" is still only 26%. It is extremely difficult to persuade people that there is no God—because there is! Even the demons know that.

But only someone with faith like that of Enoch—the faith that God gives his people—will "earnestly seek him" believing that "he rewards" those who do. Hebrews 11 is not admiring Enoch; the author is reminding his readers, including us, that, by faith, we all walk with God. The prophet Micah asks, "And what does the LORD require of you? To act justly and to love mercy and to walk humbly with your God" (Micah 6 v 8). And walking with God remains fundamental in New Testament faith. Jesus said:

> I am the light of the world. Whoever follows me will never walk in darkness, but will have the light of life.
> (John 8 v 12)

Many treasure walking in one of our many London parks with their spouse; others enjoy walking with their dog; others still with friends. But the highest privilege in life is to walk with God as we dwell upon his words in Scripture and respond in personal prayer. Are you enjoying this privilege of daily walking with God?

If you've not yet begun to walk with God, then why not pray today to the Lord Jesus—who said to a paralysed man, "Pick up your mat and walk" (Mark 2)—to heal your spiritual paralysis and help you walk with him from now on? And *if you're a Christian feeling the heat of persecution,* then pray to the Saviour who was "walking around in the fire" with the Hebrew lads who would not bow in worship to the statue of the king of Babylon, keeping them safe (Daniel 3).

When the author of Hebrews says, "He could not be found, because God had taken him away", he is reminding his readers that Enoch was taken to be with God without dying (like the prophet Elijah after him) because he'd so pleased God by his faith. So while we can expect to die normally, what an encouragement to know that God delights in our faith when we "walk in the light" (1 John 1 v 7) and "[walk] in the truth" (3 John v 4) of the gospel, in the intimate love of God.

The third example of commended faith is much more famous than Abel or Enoch...

BY FAITH NOAH OBEYED GOD'S WARNING AND INHERITED RIGHTEOUSNESS

> By faith Noah, when warned about things not seen,
> in holy fear built an ark to save his family. By his
> faith he condemned the world and became heir
> of the righteousness that is in keeping with faith.
>
> (Hebrews 11 v 7)

The writer of Hebrews 11 is still moving slowly. After Abel in Genesis 4 and Enoch in Genesis 5, he now arrives at Noah in Genesis 6. He is showing how faith has always enabled God's people to persevere. In Genesis 6 we read that the Lord saw how great human wickedness on the earth had become and that "every inclination of the thoughts of the human heart was only evil all the time" (v 5)—except for Noah. When the Lord told Noah the astonishing news that he would send a flood to judge the people of the earth, and that Noah must build a huge ark-boat 450ft (135m) long to save his family and rescue all kinds of animals and birds to repopulate the world, Noah believed him! And he showed it by obeying God's building instructions.

Can you imagine how stupid he must have seemed, telling his family and friends that a massive flood would soon destroy the known world? He must have sounded like a religious crackpot with a sandwich board reading, "WE'RE ALL DOOMED. JUDGMENT IS COMING"! Can you imagine how ridiculous he must have looked as he stopped farming and spent the family savings on timber and tools to build an enormous boat on dry land? A lot like Christians today explaining that we all need forgiveness because the gospel announces "the day when God judges people's secrets through Jesus Christ, as my gospel declares" (Romans 2 v 16).

The text says, "By his faith he condemned the world", for by accepting God's assessment of it, he distanced himself from worldly self-confident corruption and invested himself in what God said would happen, though there was absolutely no visible evidence of it happening yet! We're told twice in Genesis (6 v 9 and 7 v 1) that Noah was "righteous'" in his moral behaviour, and also that he was "blameless" in his community and, like Enoch, "walked ... with God" in his personal devotions. He wasn't perfect—we know he later sinned disgracefully. But in contrast with his community, Noah was distinctively righteous in his obedience to God. However it was never his own righteousness that saved him—for no one is good enough for heaven. In Genesis 7 we're told that God "found" (literally "saw" or "reckoned") Noah as righteous, meaning that God imputed to him the righteousness of Christ, just as with Abel and Enoch and every believer since.

The apostle Peter celebrates Noah as a "preacher of righteousness" (2 Peter 2 v 5), who commended what God desires. Hebrews 11 celebrates his "holy fear", a distinctive reverence for God. He had to swim against the tide with his politically incorrect beliefs about judgment and his ludicrous behaviour in building an ark. We have to do the same, swimming against the rising tide of corruption around us—being kind rather than cruel on social media, keeping our sexual activity for marriage, wrestling with our addictions to envy and shopping and attention-seeking and complaining. And by faith we need to live in Christ who, like the ark, is the only safe place to be when the flood of God's wrath comes upon the world to judge the living and the dead.

By such faith Noah "became heir of the righteousness that comes by faith" (NIV 84, meaning he didn't have it yet). But since the gospel promises to give Christ's perfect righteousness to all who trust him, Noah received God's *entitlement* to inherit it at the resurrection. The great thing about an inheritance is that you don't have to do anything to earn it—you just receive and enjoy it. Wonderfully, when we put our faith in Jesus, we become entitled by our heavenly Father to inherit the blessings of his Son for ever!

Noah's saving faith was expressed, not just in the fine words of worship songs on a Sunday but in the sustained and costly practical obedience of many months of building a colossal boat. If Noah had refused to build as God told him to, there would have been no ark to be saved in! This is called "the obedience that comes from faith" (Romans 1 v 5). We can't have Jesus as our Saviour without having him as our Lord. Today, faith means investing ourselves not in building an ark but, like wise men building houses on foundations of rock rather than sand, in building our lives on the rock of Christ and his teaching. So that when the Day of Judgment comes, it can be said that "the rain came down, the streams rose, and the winds blew and beat against that house; yet it did not fall, because it had foundations on the rock" (Matthew 7 v 25).

As Noah must have seemed ridiculous, and as the readers of Hebrews faced humiliation, so we can expect mockery from the world around us. But in the end Noah's trust in God was proved right when he and his family were saved. Jesus said:

> As it was in the days of Noah, so it will be at the coming of the Son of Man. For in the days before the flood, people were eating and drinking, marrying and giving in marriage, up to the day Noah entered the ark; and they knew nothing about what would happen until the flood came and took them all away. That is how it will be at the coming of the Son of Man. (Matthew 24 v 37-39)

One day, when we are all raised to face judgment, our faith in Jesus will also be vindicated.

Like Abel and Enoch, Noah was commended by God and made an heir of the righteousness that qualifies us for heaven. This faith of the ancients is ours: it is *confident, like the faith of Abel,* that God is satisfied with the blood sacrifice of Christ; *confident, like the faith of Enoch,* that God exists and rewards those who seek and walk with him; and *confident, like the faith of Noah,* that God's warnings of judgment must be taken seriously by obediently taking shelter in God's means of rescue— Christ. This is the faith God has always commended— and he commends it in us too.

3. OBEDIENT

By faith Abraham obeyed, awaited and trusted God

By faith Abraham, when called to go to a place he would later receive as his inheritance, obeyed and went, even though he did not know where he was going. By faith he made his home in the promised land like a stranger in a foreign country; he lived in tents, as did Isaac and Jacob, who were heirs with him of the same promise. For he was looking forward to the city with foundations, whose architect and builder is God. And by faith even Sarah, who was past childbearing age, was enabled to bear children because she considered him faithful who had made the promise. And so from this one man, and he as good as dead, came descendants as numerous as the stars in the sky and as countless as the sand on the seashore.

(Hebrews 11 v 8-12)

My sister and her husband went with three small children to rural Tanzania to plant gospel-teaching churches with the support of Africa Inland Mission.

Their son and his new wife are training in Kenya for doing
something similar in South Sudan with Serving in Mission.
A young couple with their new baby have just moved from
leafy Worcester Park in south London to start a new church
in Barkingside in north London. An events manager and an
operations manager enjoying lucrative careers in London
have both recently accepted roles working for our church-
planting network on a fraction of their previous salaries for
the sake of the gospel. Every year, young graduates leave
their promising career paths to become ministry trainees
and apprentices in churches across the world, learning
gospel ministry to reach the lost in a diversity of contexts.
We may well think, "I could never do that". But this text
in Hebrews 11 says to all Christians today, "You can make
amazing sacrifices—by faith!"

The author of Hebrews 11 has launched his epic series
of inspiring examples from the Old Testament of what
God has enabled his people to do by faith in him. He is
doing this to encourage his readers to persevere through
tough times. He began with "the ancients": Abel, Enoch
and Noah, who were "commended" by God. Now he offers
a more extensive reflection upon the greatest hero of faith
before Jesus—Abraham, "the father of all who believe"
(Romans 4 v 11). He reminds us of three things that God
enabled Abraham to do by his faith in God's word...

BY FAITH ABRAHAM OBEYED GOD'S COMMAND TO LEAVE HOME

By faith Abraham, when called to go to a place he
would later receive as his inheritance, obeyed and

went, even though he did not know where he was
going.   (Hebrews 11 v 8)

The life of Abraham is recounted in Genesis 11 – 25.
He grew up in a prosperous family living in the
sophisticated culture of a place called Ur of the Chaldees
in Mesopotamia (now Iraq). In Acts 7, Stephen declares,
"The God of glory appeared to our father Abraham";
God called him to leave for a foreign land, saying, "Leave
your country and your people and go to the land I will
show you", even though Abraham didn't yet know where
he was going (v 2-3).

So he, his wife Sarah and his aged father Terah packed
up and moved to Harran. It was only later in Harran,
after Terah had died, that God again spoke to Abraham,
telling him to go to the land of Canaan. Can you imagine
the extraordinary conversation back in Ur when their
bewildered neighbours dropped around to ask the old
man, Terah, why he and his household were moving?
"Terah, why are you leaving?" "Sorry, I don't know!"
"Well, who told you to go?" "Abraham says the God of
glory appeared to him and told us we must go!" "Well,
where are you going?" "I'm so sorry, we don't know that
either. We're just leaving." Can you imagine the looks on
those neighbours' faces? This sounded crazy!

Actually, this kind of obedient faith isn't unique:

As Jesus was walking beside the Sea of Galilee, he
saw two brothers, Simon called Peter and his brother
Andrew. They were casting a net into the lake, for
they were fishermen. "Come, follow me," Jesus said,

"and I will send you out to fish for people." At once
they left their nets and followed him.

(Matthew 4 v 18-20)

And later, when Peter says, "We have left everything to
follow you," Jesus replies:

No one who has left home or brothers or sisters or
mother or father or children or fields for me and the
gospel will fail to receive a hundred times as much in
this present age: homes, brothers, sisters, mothers,
children and fields—along with persecutions—and
in the age to come eternal life. (Mark 10 v 29-30)

Jesus clearly taught that to be his follower we must make
him our primary commitment. He was not suggesting
that we should abandon our love and responsibility for
our families and friends and colleagues. He was saying
that if anyone tries to prevent us from following Jesus,
we have to put him first. Following Jesus will normally
require a costly commitment of our money, time and
effort, usually in our local church; for some of us it may
mean leaving a promising career to maximise our gospel
ministry (or working for more years to finance others
to do so); or it may mean leaving our homeland to serve
gospel work abroad (or perhaps staying in a small flat to
serve the gospel in an urban centre rather than moving
out for more space in the suburbs).

God called Abraham to "leave your country and
your people", because God calls people to embrace a
new identity as his people, no longer defined by this
world's ideas of geography and race. In important

current debates about diversity, we Christians should not be asked to deny our geographic and racial heritage; we can celebrate and thank God for our different cultural backgrounds, and work against prejudice and towards respect for people of every condition, age and background, because everyone is lovingly created by God in his image and precious to him. But Christians are called to obey God's word in the Bible and, where necessary, both physically and emotionally, to leave behind our commitments to this world, including the homeland and communities we love, in obeying God for the gospel. Indeed, the New Testament word for church, *ekklesia*, means "called out".

Such faith does not demand to know what lies ahead because it trusts God. Without God, people can be very anxious about the future, desperately trying to take control of their circumstances, trying to protect themselves with all kinds of safeguards and insurance. It's been very striking, during the terrible Covid-19 global pandemic, to see how normally confident secular people have become so terribly anxious. Of course, we all have different characters. Some of us are more risk-averse than others. And I'm not suggesting that Christian faith should be foolhardy about health precautions. Christians will self-isolate and sanitise, wear seat belts and pay for insurance, accept inoculations and observe medical advice like anyone else.

But we won't feel as anxious as we once did because we know we are safe in God's sovereign plans for every day of our lives. Again, I'm not suggesting that God doesn't allow his children to suffer or get sick—many who have died of Covid-19 were Christians. But Paul explains that "we know that in all things [including suffering and death] God works for the good of those who love him ... to be conformed to the image of his Son" (Romans 8 v 28-29). God may bring suffering or sickness or persecution for his children to endure, but only and always to learn to become more like Jesus in our faith. That is comforting and brings peace to anxious hearts.

Of course, some believers do suffer from acute anxiety of many kinds, either because of their emotional make-up or because of terrible experiences in their past. We mustn't pretend that faith makes us immune from worry or assume that anxiety is sinful.

But faith in God can profoundly help because it offers reasons for feeling less anxious. Jesus says repeatedly, "Do not worry" because our Father in heaven knows what we need (Matthew 6 v 25, 31, 34); Peter says, "Humble yourselves, therefore, under God's mighty hand, that he may lift you up in due time. Cast all your anxiety on him because he cares for you" (1 Peter 5 v 6-7); and Paul says, "The Lord is near. Do not be anxious about anything, but in every situation, by prayer and petition, with thanksgiving, present your requests to God. And the peace of God, which transcends all understanding, will guard your hearts and your minds in Christ Jesus" (Philippians 4 v 5-7).

Faith in God's love and power really does help us to worry less and accept risks for him. So dwelling prayerfully upon passages about God's power and love will really help us face the future with confidence in God (for instance, Psalms 23, 46, 61, 62, 121 and 139).

And so Abraham uprooted his family and left the security and comfort of Ur for an unknown future—arriving in Harran, where his father died, far from their homeland and without knowing what God was planning. But this was not blind faith or a leap in the dark or illogical fantasy, because did you notice what Stephen said? Why did Abraham trust God enough to leave everything behind in obedience to God's word? Because "the God of glory appeared" to him! When you see the glory of God, you're willing to trust his sovereign power and loving compassion. Why did the disciples leave everything and follow Jesus? Because John the Baptist "saw Jesus coming towards him and said, 'Look, the Lamb of God, who takes away the sin of the world ... this is God's Chosen One'" (John 1 v 29, 24). When we see the spectacular glory of God supremely revealed in Jesus, we will be willing to leave everything behind to follow him. As the old hymn goes (now sung so beautifully by Lauren Daigle):

> Turn your eyes upon Jesus
> Look full in his wonderful face
> For the things of earth will grow strangely dim
> In the light of his glory and grace.

I know a couple who have moved onto a deprived housing estate to support a church-plant, even though they were told by incredulous friends, "That's no place to raise children"; and a couple who went to Uganda to teach children's workers how to explain Christ to Aids orphans;

and a young man who went to the Middle East to reach Muslims, expecting to die for Christ. These moves are physical expressions of a faith that obeys the call of God in the gospel to leave our comfort zones to follow Jesus along the way of the cross, ready to die for the salvation of others.

I suppose it's a lot like getting married. Nobody knows exactly what lies ahead. When I asked my wife, Sian, to marry me, in September 1988 on a cliff south of Sydney as the sun went down, I knew so little of what lay ahead. But I knew enough to know I could trust her—and thirty-three years of good times and hard times and five children later, I am so glad I did. The same is true in following Jesus. When my Christian father turned 80 and we had a family celebration, he stood and addressed his eighteen grand-children like this: "I want to speak to you kids—because I know the world is trying to pull you away from Christ. But I want to tell you I've been following Jesus since 1947, and I have never known a day when I had cause to regret it." He has since gone to be with his faithful Saviour.

The author's encouragement here is that if Abraham, knowing as little of God as he did, was able to leave his country and people behind, we who see so much more of the glory of God in Jesus won't mind leaving the things of this world behind for Christ. We can risk losing wealth and status, pleasure and comfort, popularity and respect to gossip the gospel with a friend. We can decide to work part-time for our church or leave a comfortable home to join a church plant, because we have surrendered by faith to obeying God's word. Whether we stay at home or move away, we can all obey God's call in the gospel to abandon our attachments to this world, take up our cross in a life of sacrificial mission for the salvation of others, and set off into the unknown to follow Jesus on a pilgrimage to his heavenly home.

BY FAITH ABRAHAM WAITED FOR GOD'S HEAVENLY CITY

> By faith he made his home in the promised land like a stranger in a foreign country; he lived in tents, as did Isaac and Jacob, who were heirs with him of the same promise. For he was looking forward to the city with foundations, whose architect and builder is God. (Hebrews 11 v 9-10)

The Lord had promised Abraham, "Go from your country, your people and your father's household to the land I will show you. I will make you into a great nation and I will bless you ... and all peoples on earth will be blessed through you" (Genesis 12 v 1-3). This promise of the earthly version of the kingdom of God is called the "gospel" in Galatians 3 v 8. Abraham believed this gospel promise and was saved, as we are saved by faith in this gospel (as it is now clarified in God's promise of his heavenly kingdom for all who accept his King, Jesus, as their Lord and Saviour). Abraham realised that the land of Canaan itself was only an earthly model of God's heavenly kingdom to come. So he lived in temporary tents like a stranger in the land, rather than buying property in Canaan and settling down. He chose not to invest in this world. He was waiting for God's permanent and heavenly city, and wanted to be part of that future. This heavenly community, God's church, is described elsewhere in Hebrews as the city "prepared by God" (chapter 11), "the city of the living God, the heavenly Jerusalem" (chapter 12), and "the city that is to come" (chapter 13).

Abraham disengaged from the place where he lived in two ways that match the description of faith in 11 v 1.

a) He lived like a stranger in a foreign land, expressing faith in the *unseen* spiritual world

Abraham wasn't desperate to fit in and put down roots. Instead of building his own house and business, he was content to live in a tent—a temporary dwelling—and his son and grandson were raised to do the same. They chose to live like gypsies or travellers or nomads with no intention of settling down. The only land Abraham bought was a tiny burial plot. He didn't mind feeling like a foreigner, an outsider, a stranger and pilgrim—because he was! Canaan was never going to feel like home to a man who longed for his true home in God's kingdom of heaven. Doesn't this challenge our culture's desire that we all own our own house or a bigger house, or that we buy or extend a holiday cottage? Some honest and prayerful reflection is appropriate before we invest funds selfishly that could have been applied to gospel ministry—and certainly when we write a will!

This is so important for us to understand as Christians because, to varying degrees, human beings like to conform and fit in—to feel we belong. The 1983 film *Zelig* (starring and produced by the disgraced genius Woody Allen), depicts a nondescript man with the ability to transform his appearance to that of people around him. He is first observed at a party interacting with affluent guests in a refined Boston accent and sharing their Republican sympathies, but then in the kitchen with the servants, adopting a coarser tone and seeming to be more of a Democrat. He soon gains international fame as a "human chameleon". The film explores the desperate need that people feel to conform and belong.

As I've previously observed, like the character Zelig, Christians feel under pressure to behave like human chameleons—gospel-focused on Sundays in church but worldly on Mondays in the office—so as to fit in and belong. Jesus warned:

> Do not store up for yourselves treasures on earth ...
> But store up for yourselves treasures in heaven,
> where moths and vermin do not destroy, and where
> thieves do not break in and steal. For where your
> treasure is, there your heart will be also.
>
> (Matthew 6 v 19-21)

Christians are tempted by the world to invest our best efforts in acquiring the material things that this world values most—property, status, education, family, pleasure, fitness and luxury. We can persuade others and deceive ourselves that the only reason we're fitting in is to evangelise unbelievers, but we won't fool God. I'm not suggesting we should be deliberately odd. Paul says, "I have become all things to all people so that by all possible means I might save some" (1 Corinthians 9 v 22). It's good to fit in with genuine friends. But the world is not our home. If you haven't explained the gospel to anyone recently, it's worth asking if you have been silenced by a desire to fit in, and then ask God for obvious opportunities to say something about Jesus.

Abraham and Jesus didn't mind feeling different because they were: challenging to the worldly maybe but compellingly distinctive to anyone interested in eternity.

b) He looked forward to the city with foundations, expressing faith in the *future* city of God

Abraham wasn't interested in any earthly city. He was more interested in the heavenly city of God! There's been a lot of wonderfully helpful thinking coming out of Tim Keller's ministry in NYC about reaching cities today. But there's also a lot of less helpful talk from elsewhere about "transforming the city". Jesus was more interested in "saving the people of the city". It's true that biblical ethics would be a rich blessing upon London, riven as it is with social problems such as broken marriages and absent fathers, substance abuse, racial injustice, knife crime, pride, wealth and poverty. And it is true that repentant Christians loving their neighbours will be a blessing to any community. But the most loving thing we can do for our city is to plant and revitalise and grow churches that proclaim salvation and the promise of the heavenly Jerusalem.

I love living in London; it's diverse, gritty, exciting, historical—the best city in the world (by far). But it's not a patch on the heavenly Jerusalem! Have you read the brochure for the heavenly Jerusalem in Revelation 21 and 22? More beautiful than Prague, more amazing than Mumbai, more exciting than New York, more relaxing than Sydney, more fun than Rio and more multicultural than London. The heavenly Jerusalem is where our God dwells in untainted, beautiful holiness—where we shall enjoy and celebrate Jesus in a more electric atmosphere than the spine-tingling roars of a Premier League football match and with more irrepressible happiness than singing along at a Coldplay concert in the Principality Stadium in Cardiff!

One influential book unhelpfully says, "We are not going somewhere else at the end of time, because this world is our home. And our home is good. One of the most tragic things to happen to the gospel was the emergence of the message that Jesus takes us somewhere else if we believe in him" (*Velvet Elvis,* Zondervan (2006), p 171). I know that the new creation will be this creation renewed, but the renewal begins with the destruction of this world by fire before its regeneration (2 Peter v 7, 10-13) and this world is not our home. John writes:

> Do not love the world or anything in the world. If anyone loves the world, love for the Father is not in them. For everything in the world—the lust of the flesh, the lust of the eyes, and the pride of life—comes not from the Father but from the world. The world and its desires pass away, but whoever does the will of God lives for ever.   (1 John 2 v 15-17)

We are to live like strangers here because our values and priorities are not of this world but of the coming kingdom. Christ-like Christians will not be enthralled by the passions of this world because they know there is better to come in the future beyond the grave. And so we don't despair when the world turns against us or keeps its baubles from us. How can we fret about not being promoted at work or invited to someone's party when we will soon be promoted to eternal glory because we are invited to the wedding feast of the King of kings? Sure—we can enjoy a daughter's wedding, a pay increase, an Emeli Sandé concert, mountain scenery, dancing the night away with friends, fine food and wine and so on—as wonderful gifts from our generous Creator, our loving heavenly Father. But they're not our goal. So if we can't have them, we're not destroyed because our goal is yet to come! In the words of the only hit song from Bachman-Turner Overdrive, "B-B-B-Baby, you just ain't seen n-n-nothin' yet!"

The faith of Abraham reminds us to remain strangers to this world and its values. We should seek the prosperity and welfare of our nations, cities and communities. But Abraham reminds us that this isn't our home. We're citizens of heaven and strangers to this world. The idolatrous greed and rebellious immorality of our earthly cities are offensive to God. The best thing we can do for London or Beijing or Lagos or Rio or Los Angeles or Santiago or Moscow or Paris is to evangelise them with the good news of the heavenly city—motivated by faith like Abraham.

We are strangers here. Our home is with God.

BY FAITH ABRAHAM TRUSTED GOD'S IMPOSSIBLE PROMISE

> And by faith even Sarah, who was past childbearing age, was enabled to bear children because she considered him faithful who had made the promise. And so from this one man, and he as good as dead, came descendants as numerous as the stars in the sky and as countless as the sand on the seashore.
>
> (Hebrews 11 v 11-12)

Abraham became the ancestor of God's people—not because he had faith to twist God's arm to do what he wanted (as if God were his personal genie in a lamp) but because, against all probability, he and his wife, Sarah, trusted God to bring life to Sarah's dead womb and give them the son he had promised.

Abraham was 100 and Sarah 90 as they wobbled around on their Zimmer frames trying to find the nappies and wipes for baby Isaac. But as Jesus reminded his disciples, "What is impossible with man is possible with God" (Luke 18 v 27). God can give life to the dead. For, as he reminded the Sadducees when they mocked the idea of resurrection from the dead, "Are you not in error because you do not know the Scriptures or the power of God?" (Mark 12 v 24)

We exercise this faith of Abraham when we maintain confidence in God's power to give life to the dead through this same gospel promise, by proclaiming it. As Abraham believed God could do the impossible, so by faith we can trust him to give new birth, even to people with the hardest and deadest of hearts, by praying for them and proclaiming the kingdom of heaven to them.

In imitating these three aspects of Abraham's faith—*obeying* God by leaving for a future country, by *waiting* for God's future city, and by *trusting* God for a future child—we too can persevere for an unseen future, by obedient faith in God's word.

4. PATIENT

By faith God's people are all waiting

*All these people were still living by faith when they died.
They did not receive the things promised; they only saw
them and welcomed them from a distance, admitting
that they were foreigners and strangers on earth. People
who say such things show that they are looking for a
country of their own. If they had been thinking of the
country they had left, they would have had opportunity to
return. Instead, they were longing for a better country—a
heavenly one. Therefore God is not ashamed to be called
their God, for he has prepared a city for them.*

(Hebrews 11 v 13-16)

The most frustratingly long journey I can remember
was in 1975 when I was growing up in Townsville
in Queensland, Australia. My parents took me and my
four younger siblings on the 1796km (1116m) journey
to the capital, Canberra, by slow goods train, which was
stiflingly hot but cheap. It took us three days to get there,

and we were fed the whole way from large Tupperware tubs of potato salad that gradually went green and tasted increasingly "fizzy".

But it was all worthwhile when we finally arrived in Canberra because I got to meet each member of the legendary touring West Indian cricket team, and got the priceless signatures of such greats as Sir Clive Lloyd, Michael Holding and the "Master Blaster" himself, Sir Vivian Richards. That journey taught me that you can endure frustratingly long periods of waiting if your expectations have been managed honestly and there is the sustaining hope of something amazing to look forward to. (I did also learn that potato salad doesn't travel well.)

I say this because at this point in Hebrews 11, the author interrupts his extensive treatment of Abraham's life of faith to emphasise some key lessons about waiting for heaven. He wants to manage his readers' expectations honestly so they'll be well prepared for the frustrations ahead—and he wants to reassure them that God's people have always reckoned that heaven is worth waiting for. He breaks off exactly here in his account of Abraham's faith because Abraham had left home for the kingdom of God but was living as a nomadic traveller in Canaan while he waited, and also because Abraham's journey by faith in God's promise functions as a pattern pointing to three future journeys of faith.

First, for the people of Israel, called by God's promise out of slavery in Egypt to journey by faith in God's word to the promised land.

Second, for our Saviour, Jesus, called by God's promise to make his "exodus" (badly translated "departure" in Luke 9 v 31) by faith in God's word through his death and resurrection to glory in heaven.

Third, for Christians, called by God's promise (Ephesians 1 v 18) to follow Jesus through life by faith in God's word to heaven.

So the writer stops here to reflect and summarise what his readers can learn from "all these people", meaning the patriarchs he's just been describing: Abraham and Sarah, Isaac and Jacob. What he is about to say is true for all Christians in every generation. He draws out five important principles for us.

1. THEY DIDN'T RECEIVED WHAT WAS PROMISED IN THIS LIFE

All these people were still living by faith when they died. They did not receive the things promised. (v 13)

To avoid disillusionment, this pastor knows it is vital to manage his readers' expectations. They needed to know that saving faith is "confidence in what we hope for" (11 v 1) beyond death, in the new creation. It is not loving to exaggerate the blessings of faith in this world. In my lifetime I have seen the pendulum swing back and forth among evangelical (Bible-obeying) churches between "under-realised eschatology" (under-emphasising the benefits of the Christian life now) and "over-realised eschatology" (over-emphasising the benefits of the Christian life now). As we shall see in the writer's next principle, living by faith in the gospel does make everything about life better now—because real hope does change the way we feel. But God has promised us a glorious future, not a glorious present. Listen to how the apostle Peter reinforces this principle:

> Praise be to the God and Father of our Lord Jesus Christ! In his great mercy he has given us new birth into a *living hope* through the resurrection of Jesus Christ from the dead, and into an *inheritance* that can never perish, spoil or fade. This inheritance is *kept in heaven for you*, who *through faith* are shielded by God's power *until the coming of the salvation* that is ready to be revealed in the last time. In all this you *greatly rejoice*, though now for a little while you may have had to *suffer grief in all kinds of trials*. These have come so that the proven genuineness of your *faith*—of greater worth than gold, which perishes even though refined by fire—may result in *praise, glory and honour when Jesus Christ is revealed*. Though you have not seen him, you love him; and even *though you do not see him now, you believe in him and are filled with an inexpressible and glorious joy*, for you are receiving the end result of your *faith*, the salvation of your souls. (1 Peter 1 v 3-9)

The Christian life of faith is full of inexpressible joy that sure and certain hope brings; but we don't yet experience the perfect health, holiness or happiness that we will in the future in heaven.

An influential church leader in Britain once foolishly wrote, "I sometimes say to people that I am not really interested in going to heaven because I am already in heaven. Heaven is where Jesus is, and if Jesus has come to live in me, things can't get much better than that ... Of course when we do leave this life, there will not be the problems we find around us here but on the inside of our lives it cannot get better than it is now, can it? It is as good as it can be ... The idea of leaving this world in order to get away from its problems, sorrows and difficulties is the attitude of the escapist" (from a booklet entitled *Eternal Destiny*, p 5).

This is, frankly, delusional and the opposite of what Hebrews says. Praise God that a wonderful surprise surely awaits that leader in the extreme joys of God's stunning new creation. Remembering the importance of honesty and truthfulness, here are two major implications.

a) Don't exaggerate the benefits of being a Christian now when *evangelising unbelievers*

In our eagerness to persuade unbelievers to become Christians, we can feel tempted to promise the kind of successful living which is only promised for heaven. But if we exaggerate in this way, unbelievers will either look at our ordinary lives and disbelieve us or give up pursuing Christianity when it doesn't deliver the success they were expecting. And since exaggeration is lying, God will not honour it. We need to find a way to talk not just about our present lives but about our future life beyond the grave, when the difference between the horrors of hell and the happiness of heaven could not be more obvious!

b) Don't exaggerate the benefits of being a Christian to other *believers*

Let's avoid exaggeration in the stories we circulate on Facebook or in counselling believers struggling with the damage of sin or the brokenness of creation in their lives. We can feel tempted to promise levels of transformation that will probably only be ours in the new creation. Yes, the love of God will improve our experience of every situation, but many of our burdens—such as struggling with mental illness and addictions, living with sickness and disability, enduring a loveless marriage or rebellious children, wrestling with narcissism, envy, lust, greed, pride or anger—while they can be lightened with a gospel perspective and improved with the help of the Holy Spirit of God, will remain with us to our dying day. We are all work in progress and the progress may be slow; so while we can promise the comforting presence, reassuring love and spiritual power of God to help us gradually change through faith in his word, let's be careful not to exaggerate what is possible now (so people don't become disillusioned) nor under-emphasise how wonderful life with God will be in heaven (so people don't give up).

For some years I counselled a heroin addict. I needed to be careful not to promise him total deliverance now from his craving any more than I could promise total deliverance now from sin, which is always addictive; but I certainly could and did promise him the deliverance and rest of heaven through Jesus.

Abraham and his family didn't receive what was promised in this life, but they most certainly will in the next! For living by faith means dying by faith—which makes death, while often a horribly miserable process, an exciting doorway into glorious joy!

2. THEY SAW AND WELCOMED WHAT WAS PROMISED – FROM A DISTANCE

> They only saw [the things promised] and welcomed them from a distance. (Hebrews 11 v 13)

Christians "live by faith, not by sight" (2 Corinthians 5 v 7) in that we don't yet fully experience the joys of heaven that we are promised. But faith does enable us to see and welcome the blessings we await from a distance. So although living by faith is not what it will be in heaven, it is still a richly experiential life.

Three times now I have been to Heathrow Airport to pick up one of my children returning home after many weeks away on some kind of gap-year travels. They are usually dishevelled, sun-tanned, exhausted and thinner, with a backpack laden with filthy clothes and ethnic artefacts. There have usually been anxious phonecalls about health issues or the need for more money, as well as exciting pictures of amazing places they've visited and extraordinary people they've met. As I've waited patiently with the crowd in the Heathrow arrivals lounge for them to finally get home safely, my joy has started long before I get to hug them! It begins to get exciting as soon as I hear the news they're coming home; it gets more exciting when the airport arrivals board reports the flight has landed; and when I can see them in the distance staggering through the doors with their baggage, my heart is ready to burst with happiness! They're not home yet, but seeing them in the distance makes everything better. That's what faith does. Christ is still in heaven—but we've heard the news in the gospel that he's coming back; our faith helps us see him and welcome him with excitement even before he actually gets here. That's why churches that teach genuine faith in the gospel will not be promising wealth and healing now but they will be filled with excitement and irrepressible joy—because by faith we can see him coming!

However, in the meantime...

3. THEY LIVED AS FOREIGNERS AND STRANGERS – ON EARTH

> ... admitting that they were foreigners and strangers on earth.   (Hebrews 11 v 13)

We've already explored how Christians looking forward to God's heavenly kingdom of righteousness cannot feel entirely at home or permanently invested in this dark world. This theme of God's people being "foreigners and strangers"—outsiders and nomads in this world because our home is now in the next—is emphasised in the Bible in four stages.

a) When Abraham bought a small plot of land at Hebron in which to bury his wife, Sarah, he said to the Hittite landowners, "I am a foreigner and stranger among you" (Genesis 23 v 4). He recognised that in following the call of God to his heavenly city, his life in Canaan was strictly temporary. He was just passing through like a nomadic gypsy. In the same way, we are to live as strangers and pilgrims passing through this world.

b) However, when the people of Israel returned to inherit the promised land, no longer as strangers, when David was king of Israel, he described his life in Jerusalem in the presence of God like this: "I dwell with you as a foreigner, a stranger, as all my ancestors were" (Psalm 39 v 12). And at the dedication of the temple in Jerusalem, his son, King Solomon, expressed his wonder at the grace of the Lord towards his people, saying, "We are foreigners and strangers in your sight, as were all our ancestors" (1 Chronicles 29 v 15). We too should recognise that in our sin we were once foreigners and strangers to God and have been welcomed into his presence only by his amazing grace. And so...

c) Jesus was treated like a foreigner and stranger by the Jewish leaders who hated him and accused him of being "a Samaritan and demon-possessed" (John 8 v 48) (that is, a foreigner who came from the devil), and had him crucified outside the city wall, where, on the cross, he was excluded from his Father's presence for our sin. Which is to say, Jesus took our place as a foreigner and stranger to God, so that in his place, whatever our background, we are now insiders, welcomed into the home of the living God in heaven. So...

d) Christians are now called, like Jesus, to live as foreigners and strangers in a sinful world—"Dear friends, I urge you, as foreigners and exiles, to abstain from sinful desire, which war against your soul" (1 Peter 2 v 11)—but no longer as foreigners and strangers to God: "You are no longer foreigners and strangers, but fellow citizens with God's people and also members of his household" (Ephesians 2 v 19).

Home is where we feel safe to be ourselves; we kick off our shoes, play the music we really like at full volume (for me it's Pink Floyd, the Eagles, Coldplay and Adele) and relax. Through faith in the gospel of Christ and him crucified, having once belonged in this world—and so been strangers to God, excluded from heaven—we are now strangers and gypsies passing through this world as we wait to be welcomed into our new home in heaven. There we can relax with Jesus and all our brothers and sisters, home at last. So...

4. THEY WERE LOOKING FORWARD TO THEIR OWN COUNTRY — HEAVEN

> People who say such things show that they are looking for a country of their own. If they had been thinking of the country they had left, they would have had opportunity to return.
>
> (Hebrews 11 v 14-15)

I don't think Christians can be overly nationalistic because we are looking forward to our own country in heaven, where we belong. This is not to diminish the joy of our particular cultural history or to criticise our emotional attachments to our homeland. So, as Koreans feel nostalgic about the green mountains of their homeland, and Australians feel nostalgic about the vastness of the bush, and Kenyans celebrate the red soil of their land, I admit to feeling a little sentimental when the ferry from Europe approaches the white cliffs of Dover. But, Christians will always feel frustrated by the godlessness of our national governments and media because earthly nations are not run in accordance with the word of God as heaven is. Heaven is our homeland now.

And I don't think Christians can fully buy into the politics of "intersectionality" which is currently emerging in our society. This is the notion that when we've experienced injustice in our lives, we are bound to stand with every other group who feel victimised, because if we don't, we will have betrayed who we are. Which is to surrender to the notion that our identity is forever trapped in being a victim with the right and duty to angrily protest and deconstruct authority (at its root a Marxist political idea).

Christians will certainly want to work and campaign for justice and compassion where we can: for example, for racial justice and against abortion. And we will want to show compassionate love for people in all their physical and emotional needs. (Living in London, I often find myself trying to help Christian asylum seekers.)

But Christians know that the greatest need of London or anywhere is for salvation through evangelism and not social justice through political action. And our churches are for equipping us in this work of making disciples of all nations for Jesus, not for trying to solve the social problems all around us. Please don't mishear me. Jesus told us to be like the Good Samaritan, loving those we meet in need in any way we can. But don't forget that the most loving thing we can do for anyone is to bring them to Jesus. And when Jesus turned from healing to preaching, and then told the paralysed man, "Your sins are forgiven", it was because the greatest need of humanity is the forgiveness of sins (Mark 1 v 38; 2 v 5).

Since our home is not London, or any earthly city, but the heavenly Jerusalem of God, we will want to love people in every way we can—but especially with evangelism that brings people of all nations to their new home in the kingdom of heaven.

If Abraham and his family had passionately identified as citizens of Ur of the Chaldees in Mesopotamia, from which they had come, they were free to return! But they didn't because the Lord had awoken in them longings for the kingdom of God; and there was no going back. Wonderfully...

5. GOD IS NOT ASHAMED OF THOSE WHO LIVE BY FAITH – HE'S PREPARED A CITY FOR THEM

Instead, they were longing for a better country—a heavenly one. Therefore God is not ashamed to be called their God, for he has prepared a city for them.

(Hebrews 11 v 16)

Living by faith is a life of "longing"—elsewhere described as *waiting* and *groaning*. "You turned to God from idols to serve the living and true God, and to wait for his Son from heaven" and "We ourselves ... groan inwardly as we wait eagerly for our adoption to sonship, the redemption of our bodies. For in this hope we were saved. But hope that is seen is no hope at all" (1 Thessalonians 1 v 9-10; Romans 8 v 23-24). So while we delight in God in Christ in the Spirit now, there will always be a sense of quiet frustration and lament which is part of the hope for the kingdom of heaven created by God in our hearts by the gospel. Astonishingly, God is unashamed of us.

Notice in Hebrews 11 v 16 that this is for two reasons: one is indicated by the subsequent word "therefore", which is that by faith we are longing to see him. The other reason why he is unashamed, indicated by the preceding word "for", is that he has prepared a glorious heavenly city at the cost of his Son's death on a cross for us. God is not only pleased that we want to be with him but pleased that his plan to provide a new home for us will be wonderfully fulfilled.

Imagine a good man who falls in love with a woman who has previously been wayward but who now recognises in him her chance of lasting love. While he unhurriedly dates and gets to know her, he secretly spends every spare moment, and all the money he has, on refurbishing and refurnishing his house in beautiful ways which he knows she will love, confident that they will one day be married. When he finally asks her on bended knee to marry him, she replies with tears of joy, "Oh my love, yes! I've been longing for you to ask me. I want to spend the rest of my life with you." To which he joyfully responds, "I am so happy to marry you—first because you want me, and second because I've invested everything I have in a beautiful new home for us to be happy in together. Come and see!" God has prepared not just a beautiful house but a whole stunningly beautiful city: "It shone with the glory of God, and its brilliance was like that of a very precious jewel" (Revelation 21 v 11). The Bridegroom of the church, our loving Saviour, Jesus, can't wait to show us around the city he has prepared for us!

The simple lesson for us today is that living by faith requires us to be *patient*—to feel like strangers and foreigners in this world because we are longing for heaven, waiting and groaning for the marvellous heavenly city God has prepared for us. We can stop complaining about the hardships we face and stop expecting things to be perfect now, in our friendships, our careers, our social life, our marriages and our churches. The eternal joys of life in heaven will make the temporary costs of being a Christian on earth seem trifling.

I live in south-west London, not far from the famous Wimbledon Tennis Championships courts. When we first moved here, I discovered that many tennis fans will queue all night on the pavements outside the courts, waiting for affordable tickets into this most prestigious of tournaments. What on earth could persuade people to wait all night like that? Can tennis really ever be that interesting? When I finally experienced the excitement and glamour of a day at Wimbledon for myself, I understood why it was worth waiting all night. The glamour and excitement of being with Jesus will make Wimbledon seem dull by comparison.

Be patient. Keep waiting by faith. The best is definitely yet to come—and will make all the waiting worthwhile!

5. SACRIFICIAL

By faith Abraham made an extreme sacrifice

*By faith Abraham, when God tested him, offered Isaac
as a sacrifice. He who had embraced the promises was
about to sacrifice his one and only son, even though God
had said to him, "It is through Isaac that your offspring
will be reckoned." Abraham reasoned that God could
even raise the dead, and so in a manner of speaking he
did receive Isaac back from death.*

(Hebrews 11 v 17-19)

In Jerusalem today, within the Dome of the Rock, built
by Muslims in AD 691 upon the site of Solomon's
temple, lies an exposed slab of rock. It is venerated by
visiting pilgrims as the place where Abraham was willing
to sacrifice his son. Muslims celebrate this event in their
feast of Eid ul-Adha, and Jews still celebrate the "binding
of Isaac". Hebrews 11 reminds weary Christians of this
astonishing act of faith to encourage us to see that God
can empower extraordinary sacrifice through faith in him.

As we've seen, Hebrews is a beautifully crafted sermon from an unknown learned pastor to discouraged Jewish believers facing hostility, confiscation of property and physical persecution for their faith. They were tempted to shrink back from their public witness, just as Christians everywhere are under pressure to keep quiet about Jesus. In Western secular cultures there's an increasingly intolerant and "muscular" liberal ideology under which Christians are openly despised or even required to undergo "diversity training" if we won't espouse its *woke* agendas because they contradict the teachings of Jesus (for example, on gender fluidity or same-sex marriage). In the Middle East, the act of evangelising Muslims can bring beatings, prison or execution. In totalitarian states, Christians face summary arrest, labour camp and/or death. How can Christians facing such hostility remain loyal to Christ?

Most of us in the West are very unlikely to face a beating, but we find being criticised or ostracised very painful, and initiating conversations about Jesus, or even just telling our story, feels difficult. Where will we find the costly courage to "let [our] light shine before others, that they may see [our] good deeds and glorify [our] Father in heaven" (Matthew 5 v 16)? Where can we find the strength to risk our popularity to speak up for God or invite people to church?

The author is accumulating his "cloud of witnesses" (12 v 1) to testify that God can empower his readers to persevere by faith in his word. Having reminded them of the "ancients—Abel, Enoch and Noah—the author has drawn lessons from the faith of the "patriarchs", chief among them Abraham. He now focuses upon one extraordinary event recorded in Genesis 22. The Lord tested Abraham's faith by asking him to sacrifice his beloved son, Isaac. The writer is demonstrating that God has *always* empowered his people to make extreme sacrifices—by faith in him. He identifies three things that God enabled Abraham to do...

BY FAITH ABRAHAM WAS WILLING TO SACRIFICE HIS BELOVED SON

> By faith Abraham, when God tested him, offered
> Isaac as a sacrifice.   (Hebrews 11 v 17)

At the climax to Abraham's life, we read in Genesis 22 of the Lord *testing* Abraham's faith in him, by asking him to sacrifice what was most precious in all the world to him—his son, Isaac. We are told in the account what Abraham was not told—that this was not a command to commit murder but a test to strengthen Abraham's faith. For while Satan tests (meaning *tempts*) our faith in God's word, hoping to get us to abandon it, the Lord only tests (same word but meaning *trains*) our faith to strengthen it, like an athlete stressing a muscle group. Any challenge in life will offer both Satan's temptation to abandon God and God's training in trusting God. What God requires of us in his word may sometimes be perplexing and often costly. Like Abraham, we need to learn to trust God's goodness and wisdom in all the events of our lives.

When Abraham heard God's call, he responded with the submissive words of Samuel, David, Isaiah and Jesus

(Hebrews 10 v 7; Genesis 22 v 1): "Here I am". Then came God's astonishing instruction in words structured to emphasise the terrible cost: "Take your son, your only son, whom you love—Isaac—and go to the region of Moriah. Sacrifice him there as a burnt offering" (Genesis 22 v 2). Amazingly, Abraham's faith in God was once again expressed in obedience, despite the immense personal cost and despite the confusing implications.

ABRAHAM OBEYED GOD DESPITE THE IMMENSE PERSONAL COST

We can hardly begin to imagine the anguish in Abraham's heart. Although Abraham had another son, called Ishmael, by Hagar, it was Isaac who had been miraculously born to Sarah in fulfilment of God's promise—to give Abraham descendants from whom the Saviour of the world would come. Of course, we can read the account knowing that God has actually now done this himself in surrendering his only beloved Son, Jesus, to die for us. But Abraham didn't know this. Imagine the tears streaming down his face as he led his little boy up the hill, especially when Isaac asked him anxiously, "Father? The fire and wood are here, but where is the lamb for the burnt offering?" (Genesis 22 v 7)

However, there is a big clue in the text that Abraham had already worked out that somehow this would not be the end for Isaac. For in the text of Genesis 22, Abraham says something extraordinary to the servants left behind to care for the donkey. "Stay here with the donkey while I and the boy go over there. *We* will worship and then *we* will come back to you" (v 5). The writer to the Hebrews is about to tell us that Abraham assumed that Isaac would be raised from the dead. But it's hard to think he could have been very confident about this, and it would still have meant him having to kill Isaac! Abraham was probably also already wondering if God would provide a substitute, for he answered Isaac's question strangely: "God himself will provide the lamb" (v 8). No doubt his anguished mind was a bewildered tangle of questions.

But having climbed the hill together, engulfed by anxiety and dread, they got to the point where Abraham had to lay down his son on the altar and lift his knife to strike. That's when the angel of the LORD intervened, saying:

> "Now I know that you fear God, because you have not withheld from me your son, your only son."
>
> Abraham looked up and there in a thicket was a ram caught by its horns. He went over and took the ram and sacrificed it as a burnt offering instead of his son. So Abraham called that place The LORD Will Provide. (Genesis 22 v 12-14)

Child sacrifice was tragically a feature of many pagan religions in Abraham's day. But God's word condemns all child sacrifice (Deuteronomy 18 v 10) and so most Christians everywhere urgently want to reduce the appalling abortion rates of the 21st century. On 13th June 2019, the *Independent* newspaper reported, "The number of abortions in England and Wales has reached a record high of more than 200,000 in a year—with older women and mothers behind the rise ... There were 200,608 abortions for women resident in England and Wales in

2018—up 4 per cent on the 192,900 the previous year." We will surely look back one day, as we now look back on the slave trade, and ask, "How could so many Christians have turned a blind eye and done nothing about that?"

And Christians will obviously want to vigorously support the safeguarding of all children (and adults at risk). So it is disturbing to think of God even suggesting, and Abraham being willing, to kill Isaac. Hebrews 11 says Abraham was assuming Isaac's resurrection, and the text of Genesis says he was also assuming God's provision of a substitute. But it's still alarming to read of our holy God ever telling Abraham to kill his son when he condemns child sacrifice so strongly elsewhere. Perhaps it's helpful to remember that not only did God always intend to protect Isaac, but, uniquely in God's plans for salvation, Isaac was God's miraculous gift, and he was consecrated to God when he was circumcised. In the end, it is God who takes the life of everyone when we die, which is his unique right as our Creator and Judge. Clearly it was part of God's testing to see if Abraham could trust the goodness of God even when the command sounded appalling.

A REHEARSAL FOR THE SACRIFICE OF JESUS

Mount Moriah was actually the very hill on which Jerusalem and the temple would later be built, and where Jesus would be sacrificed for our sins. The provision of a substitutionary sacrifice for Isaac foreshadowed not just the animal sacrifices of the temple but the ultimate sacrifice of Christ on the cross for our sins. There are four aspects to this traumatic event which foreshadow the death of Jesus.

First, the journey up the hill looked forward not only to Israel's journey up Mount Sinai to make sacrifices but to Christ's ascent to his place of crucifixion, carrying not firewood but the wooden beam to which he was nailed for our sins.

Second, the provision of a ram in a thicket prefigures not only the Passover lambs killed to satisfy the Lord when he "passed over" Israel in his judgment of Egypt, but it also prefigures Jesus, "the Lamb of God, who takes away the sin of the world" (John 1 v 29), and who died crowned with thorns on a cross.

Third, Abraham's willingness to sacrifice his beloved son, rewarded by receiving him back as if from the dead, foreshadows the love of God. As we contemplate the horror of this episode, we begin to better grasp what our Father in heaven did at the cross, in giving his precious Son to suffer for us before receiving him back by resurrection. His love for you and me is truly astonishing.

And *fourth*, as the sacrifice on Mount Moriah secured for Abraham the covenant promise of many descendants through whom a Saviour would come for people of all nations, so Christ's blood secured for us the blessings of the new covenant, based upon the forgiveness of our sins. As Abraham was confirmed by his faith to be the ancestor of countless physical descendants, so Jesus was confirmed by his self-sacrifice to be the founder of a vast new spiritual people from all nations.

The whole episode at Mount Moriah was arranged by God to help show us what he was prepared to give for us. Like Abraham, God the Father would surrender his beloved Son to death. But unlike Isaac, who was a helpless child, Jesus volunteered for death trusting his Father's promise of resurrection, by faith. Jesus' faith was like Abraham's faith.

So when Jesus calls us to deny ourselves, take up our cross and follow him, there may be great personal costs involved. Dietrich Bonhoeffer, the German pastor imprisoned and finally executed for his opposition to Hitler and Nazism, wrote about this from prison in letters collected together and published as *The Cost of Discipleship*. "The cross is laid on every Christian," he wrote. "When Christ calls a man, he bids him come and die ... Suffering then, is the badge of true discipleship. The disciple is not above his master ... That is why Luther reckoned suffering among the marks of the true church ... If we refuse to take up our cross and submit to suffering and rejection at the hands of men, we forfeit our fellowship with Christ and have ceased to follow him."

Do you remember what Peter tells his persecuted readers? "For a little while you may have had to suffer grief in all kinds of trials. These have come so that the proven genuineness of your faith—of greater worth than gold, which perishes even though refined by fire—may result in praise, glory and honour when Jesus Christ is revealed" (1 Peter 1 v 6-7). Such trials may include giving up an ungodly relationship ourselves. Or, perhaps harder, watching our children make self-sacrifices as they follow Jesus down the road of the cross—perhaps risking a reprimand at work for evangelising colleagues, or leaving a popular career to go into paid gospel ministry as a ministry trainee, or leaving home to become a Bible translator in a distant land. Faith in the goodness of God will empower us to obey his commands whatever the personal cost.

Abraham had a unique role in salvation history, and there is no reason for us to expect such an extreme sacrifice. But God will bring appropriate testing to every follower of Jesus at some point. And this passage reassures us that God will give us the faith we need to make whatever sacrifice God thinks is good for us in becoming like Jesus. Listen to what Joni Eareckson Tada says about her diving accident at the age of 17, which left her living with quadriplegia: "Suffering provides the gym equipment on which my faith can be exercised ... He has chosen not to heal me, but to hold me. The more intense the pain, the closer his embrace ... So here I sit ... glad that I have not been healed on the outside, but glad that I have been healed on the inside. Healed from my own self-centred wants and wishes ... Maybe the truly handicapped people are the ones that don't need God as much—this paralysis is my greatest mercy" (see "Joni Eareckson Tada Quotes" online). Can you hear how God has given Joni the faith she needs to sacrifice her expectations of health because she values forgiveness and knowing God by faith more highly? That is like Abraham's faith.

ABRAHAM BELIEVED GOD DESPITE THE CONFUSING IMPLICATIONS

He who had embraced the promises was about to sacrifice his one and only son, even though God had said to him, "It is through Isaac that your offspring will be reckoned." Abraham reasoned that God could even raise the dead, and so in a manner of speaking he did receive Isaac back from death. (v 17-19)

God had promised Abraham that a nation would arise from his descendants. So for Abraham to sacrifice his precious son—the miracle baby given to Abraham and Sarah in their old age—must have seemed like madness! How could God keep his promise of many descendants if Isaac were killed?

Abraham's willingness to sacrifice Isaac illustrates how faith has always enabled God's people to do things that seem contradictory to our own logic because we trust that God knows best. For example, Jesus said, "For whoever wants to save their life will lose it, but whoever loses their life for me and for the gospel will save it" (Mark 8 v 35). This sounds nonsensical: how can giving away our life to Jesus mean we save it? There are many things in the Bible that sound confusing unless we have faith to trust that God knows better than us!

It's a bit like obeying an experienced ski instructor, who will tell you that on a steep, icy mountain slope you must do the opposite of what feels sensible. Everything in your terrified mind makes you want to lean towards the hill, but this makes your skis slide away. You have to learn to trust the ski instructor and lean away from the hill, which surprisingly keeps your skis cutting into the mountain slope to keep you safe. At the beginning, I can tell you from experience, this feels frightening and confusing—but you have to trust the instructor. In the same way, faith enables us to obey God's word even if it seems confusing or impossible.

Abraham didn't just talk about faith like this; he *lived* by it. James observes, "Was not our father Abraham considered righteous *for what he did* when he offered Isaac on the altar? You see that his faith and his actions were working together, and his faith was made complete by what he did. And the scripture was fulfilled that says, 'Abraham believed God, and it was credited to him as righteousness,' and he was called God's friend" (James 2 v 21-23). Saving faith is expressed and completed in action, however costly. Abraham didn't just claim to have faith or just sing about his faith. He *obeyed* in faith, at great cost to himself and to those he loved, and so he was regarded by God as his "friend". Do you want to be God's friend? Live by faith in his word!

Abraham's faith wasn't a blind faith or a leap in the dark. On the contrary, he "reasoned"—he reflected upon God's command and thought about God's promise and concluded correctly that, since God would certainly keep his promise of descendants through Isaac *and* that God's command to kill Isaac must be obeyed, the only explanation was... resurrection. When Abraham told the servants, "We will worship and then we will come back to you", he wasn't a liar but a believer. Despite the apparent impossibility, by faith he knew that the Lord would never fail to keep his promise and, "in a manner of speaking he did receive Isaac back from death" (Hebrews 11 v 19).

Christian faith is not unreasonable. Abraham *reasoned*. God wants reasoning faith, not make-believe faith. But

Christian faith also embraces the supernatural power of God. So like Abraham, Christians consistently believe the gospel promise of bodily resurrection: "For we believe that Jesus died and rose again, and so we believe that God will bring with Jesus those who have fallen asleep in him" (1 Thessalonians 4 v 14).

WE NEED TO ENABLE OUR FAMILIES TO MAKE SACRIFICES FOR GOD

Abraham's faith involved his wife and son in his costly sacrifice for God. Sometimes we try to protect those we love from the costs of following Jesus. But living by faith may require us to involve our family in the costs of ministry, and we should not be frightened to explain this and invite them to share in the blessing of making sacrifices for Jesus. We need to help them understand that remaining in a small urban apartment to support a faithful local church, rather than follow the crowd towards a bigger house in the suburbs, will mean sacrifices for the whole family. We need to help our spouse understand that accepting a lesser-paid job may offer better working hours to enable us to be home for homegroup; they need to know that sacrificial generosity in financing gospel work will mean more ordinary holidays and fewer clothes or gadgets for all of us. We may need to explain to our children why we are removing them from godless sex-education classes at school or to insist that they come to church most Sundays instead of playing football like their friends. Sacrificial service of God is good for kids as well as adults. It helps them to clarify their faith as well as us to clarify ours.

But we can't claim that our obedience is sacrificial until it hurts. This is not to look for pointless sacrificial pain. Pain is not good, and God forbids asceticism: the refusal to enjoy the generosity of God. Indeed, it is demonic to forbid the biblical, thankful enjoyment of God's good creation (1 Timothy 4 v 4). Jesus was not a sado-masochist. He didn't go to the cross because he enjoyed pain. He went to the cross because there was no other way to save sinners. Likewise, in following him, God will give us the faith we need to suffer where it is necessary in obedience to God for the salvation of others.

FAITH LIKE ABRAHAM'S WILL HELP US DIE WITH CONFIDENCE

God gives his people faith like that of Abraham so we can die in full assurance of the reality of heaven. *Killing Fields, Living Fields* is a moving account of the Christian church in Cambodia during the horrific oppression of the Khmer Rouge under Pol Pot in the 1970s, when 70% of the Christians were slaughtered. The author, Don Cormack, describes the execution—one of many—of a Christian family led by a man called Haim. The faith of this man reveals the practical confidence of Christian faith in bodily resurrection, like that of Abraham.

A sickly smell of death hung in the air. Curious villagers foraging in the scrub nearby lingered, half hidden, watching the familiar routine as the family were ordered to dig a large grave for themselves. Then, consenting to Haim's request for a moment to prepare themselves for death, father, mother, and children, hands linked, knelt together around the gaping pit. With loud cries to God, Haim began exhorting both the Khmer Rouge and all those looking on from afar to repent and believe the gospel. Then in panic, one of Haim's young sons leapt to his feet, bolted into the surrounding bush and disappeared. Haim jumped up and with amazing coolness and authority prevailed upon the Khmer Rouge not to pursue the lad, but to allow him to call the boy back. The knots of onlookers, peering around trees, the Khmer Rouge, and the stunned family still kneeling at the graveside, looked on in awe as Haim began calling his son, pleading with him to return and die together with his family. "What comparison, my son," he called out, "stealing a few more days of life in the wilderness, a fugitive, wretched and alone, to joining your family here momentarily around this grave but soon around the throne of God, free forever in Paradise?" After a few tense minutes the bushes parted, and the lad, weeping, walked slowly back to his place with the kneeling family. "Now we are ready to go," said Haim to the Khmer Rouge. The family were all killed, their bodies toppling into the grave, but their souls released into the presence of Jesus for ever.

Such behaviour will seem like madness to the unsaved, who have no hope of heaven. But God gives to all his people this faith in the future unseen reality of resurrection life—not just to Abraham but to us too!

So we too can make the sacrifices for God we didn't think we could make—by faith.

6. ASPIRATIONAL

By faith the patriarchs planned for life after death

By faith Isaac blessed Jacob and Esau in regard to their future. By faith Jacob, when he was dying, blessed each of Joseph's sons, and worshipped as he leaned on the top of his staff. By faith Joseph, when his end was near, spoke about the exodus of the Israelites from Egypt and gave instructions concerning the burial of his bones.

(Hebrews 11 v 20-22)

What aspirations and hopes do you have for your children or grandchildren or the children of your church family? Promoting a book by Dr. Wayne W. Dyer, *What Do You Really Want For Your Children?*, the Amazon website observes, "All parents have the same dream for their children—that they grow up happy, healthy, self-reliant, and confident in themselves and their abilities. Now Dr Wayne W. Dyer uses the same dynamic techniques that fired his previous multimillion-copy bestsellers to show us how to make those special dreams for our kids come true." But how does faith in Christ affect our aspirations for our children?

After all, the readers of Hebrews 11 would have been worried sick about the effects on their own kids, and on the children of their church families, of the hostility and persecution they were facing for their faith in Christ. One of the most common reasons why Christians shrink back from evangelism and public loyalty to the teaching of Christ is the desire to protect their children from hostility at school. One of my own children once arrived at school to find a posse of her classmates waiting to interrogate her view of same-sex marriage. When she nervously admitted that she wasn't in favour, they announced with a hostility which they must have picked up from their parents, "We think that's terrible! This changes everything! Is that what your father thinks? We're never coming to your church!" She fled from the scene in tears and was cold-shouldered all day. When I later piously suggested, "Honey, I guess this is your first taste of suffering for Jesus, which means you are blessed by God," she responded with some force, "Dad, it feels like a lot more than a taste—more like a whole meal!"

Of course, in many cultures the cost of being Christian is much more serious. *Christianity Today* magazine has reported, "Christians in North Korea face rape, torture, enslavement, and being killed for their faith, a damning new report from Christian Solidarity Worldwide (CSW) has warned. Religious beliefs are seen as a threat to the loyalty demanded by the Supreme Leader, so anyone holding these beliefs is severely persecuted." Among the documented crimes against Christians are "being hung on a cross over a fire, crushed under a road roller, herded off bridges and trampled underfoot" (*Christianity Today*, 23rd September 2016). That is just what it was like for Christians during outbreaks of persecution in the Roman Empire.

Christian parents, then and now, obviously want to protect their children. But if faith is "'confidence in what we hope for and assurance about what we do not see" (11 v 1)—confidence in God's gospel promise of an inheritance in the heavenly kingdom of God—we will surely want much more for our kids than tennis lessons, a happy marriage and a rewarding career. We'll want them to know Christ and inherit heaven with us! We'll want to encourage them to live by faith.

This is what we find in the brief descriptions of the faith of the patriarchs Isaac, Jacob and Joseph. It's often missed that these verses describe not only what they wanted beyond the grave for themselves but what they wanted for their children and grandchildren. Here are three examples of how God empowered faith in ordinary people (some of whom failed spectacularly in their lives) to trust God to keep his gospel promise beyond their own death; and of how faith enabled them to commend this gospel to the next generation. Each did so with a blessing—a kind of prayer that expresses hopes for someone else in the presence of God—when their families gathered to be with them shortly before they died. We must all die one day, and faith in Christ prepares us well for that.

Let's consider each patriarch in turn...

ISAAC

> By faith Isaac blessed Jacob and Esau in regard to
> their future. (Hebrews 11 v 20)

Isaac was a foolish man. He even once abandoned his wife, Rebekah, to save his own skin (Genesis 26 v 7)! But in his old age when he was blind—despite being tricked by Rebekah into blessing her favourite son, Jacob, rather than his older brother, Esau—even Isaac knew that God would one day keep his promise to bring his descendants into the promised land.

Abraham, Isaac and Jacob realised that the earthly promise made to them—the promise of God's people inheriting God's land to enjoy God's blessing and bring blessing to all nations (Genesis 12 v 1-3)—was the pledge of something far greater. It was the pledge of the gospel of Christ—God's blessing for all nations—being taken by world mission to sinners of all nations, calling them to enjoy God's blessing together in heaven. So, by faith in God, Isaac prayed for his sons to benefit from this gospel.

We find the dramatic occasion of this blessing recorded in Genesis 27. Being blind, Isaac didn't realise that he'd been tricked by Rebekah into blessing Jacob instead of the older brother Esau (a blessing that God allowed because he wanted the son who couldn't expect to inherit to benefit from his promise—to illustrate how he now saves undeserving sinners like us entirely by grace).

Isaac begins by praying, as you might expect, for prosperity and happiness: "May God give you heaven's dew and earth's richness—an abundance of grain and new wine". As in Jesus' Lord's Prayer, encouraging us to ask for our "daily bread"—which includes asking for our material needs as well as the spiritual food of his word—mature Christians will rightly ask for material provision from our Creator.

But then Isaac prays in accordance with God's promise: "May nations serve you and peoples bow down to you ... May those who curse you be cursed and those who bless you be blessed." At first this just sounds like a prayer for success. But the words reflect something of God's promise to Rebekah when the boys were born (Genesis 25 v 23), and will be fulfilled in their descendant Jesus, the Lord who will rule and bless his people from all nations. Isaac is praying, in accordance with God's word, for his son to be part of God's future kingdom.

Faith enables Christians to pray with gospel priorities like this. My own recently deceased parents were both born again as young adults: my father through a local youth group and my mother through the amazing Billy Graham mission at Harringay Arena, London, in 1954 (when two million people attended evening rallies and 40,000 people responded to the call of Christ). My father took early retirement from being a university professor to spend twenty years offering himself as a Bible teacher free of charge to a series of churches. My parents paid for this by repeatedly downsizing their house (in contrast with so many who hoard their wealth). My parents weren't perfect, but what I and my siblings most value about them is that they prayed for us nearly every night and struggled with us at every evening meal to read some portion of Scripture and pray together. The most precious thing our parents gave us was the gospel and their prayers: the most valuable inheritance there is.

Isaac reminds us that however sinful and foolish we've been in our lives, it's never too late to be a blessing to our children and grandchildren in praying gospel prayers for them—not only for their prosperity and happiness but for them to believe and proclaim the gospel as citizens of God's heavenly kingdom.

JACOB

> By faith Jacob, when he was dying, blessed each of Joseph's sons, and worshipped as he leaned on the top of his staff.   (Hebrews 11 v 21)

As Jacob was dying, he stubbornly blessed his younger grandson first (Genesis 48 v 13-14), presumably again to emphasise that blessing comes not by human lineage but by God's grace. In his blessing, by faith he reassured his son Joseph: "I am about to die, but God will be with you and take you back [from Egypt] to the land of your fathers" (48 v 21). By faith, he too believed that God would keep his gospel promise. The reference to Jacob worshipping as he leaned on his staff is to emphasise that, at the end of his life, Jacob was trusting the Lord to bring him through death into his presence.

I recall when I was a young minister being asked to visit an elderly Christian lady called Vera, who was dying in hospital. Not knowing her but aware of my responsibility to share the gospel with her, I gently asked, "Vera, are you trusting in Jesus' death for your sins to save you into heaven?" She was lying on her side and too weak to move, but replied with surprising confidence and a smile, "Of course I am—he's the only chance I've got!" That is the faith of Jacob that can die with confidence.

Jacob goes further than his father, Isaac. He prays for his grandsons: "May the God before whom my fathers Abraham and Isaac walked faithfully, the God who has been my shepherd all my life to this day, the Angel who has delivered me from all harm—may he bless these boys" (48 v 15-16). He is testifying to the Lord being his guiding shepherd and guardian angel—asking God to be the same for his grandsons. Jacob then prays blessings for each of his sons in turn. When he prays for the tribe of Judah, he prays in accordance with God's gospel promise: "The sceptre will not depart from Judah until he to whom it belongs shall come [Jesus] and the obedience of the nations shall be his" (Genesis 49 v 10). He is expressing his hope in the coming of God's Messiah, Jesus—who would come from the family line of Judah—in accordance with the promise made to his grandfather, Abraham.

By faith, if we have children, we can do something similar. Husband and wife can take it in turns to read a children's Bible and then share prayer requests with our kids for 5-10 minutes at a mealtime or at bedtime when they are young (though after school years this may be best left to their own time with God). Though kids might increasingly protest as they get older and want to escape to the TV or homework, my children look back on those Bible times with great fondness. Indeed, we parents, who may feel we get very little else right in parenting, can get this supremely important thing right if we try. It's worth discussing it and agreeing mutual support with our spouse.

We can share our faith with our grandchildren when we cook meals or go fishing or share a holiday with them, even if an unbelieving son or daughter–in-law makes it difficult to do so at mealtimes. We can pray for them whenever we give thanks for a meal ("say grace") and on birthdays, when they triumph and when they are worried, and before a long journey, however old our children or grandchildren are.

No one is saved by good parenting or grandparenting but only by God's grace. I have a friend who is the coolest and most dedicated Christian dad you can imagine; he ran a huge youth ministry and read the Bible and prayed with his family every day at the dinner table. If anyone can be saved by parenting, it would be his kids. But only one of his four kids is professing faith in Christ. I try to remind him that the battle for their souls has only just begun.

And yet, by God's grace alone, kids who are prayed for and read with do seem to become Christians more often. I think it's not just the content of the passages we read that is so compelling for kids. I think children are persuaded to listen when they experience their parents trying to insist on something because they genuinely believe it to be true. Children see our convictions in what we do, so if we can't be bothered to care about their faith, then why should they?

And we can have a surprising influence upon the children of friends. Certainly my experience is that even if young people are more mature and independent than ever, they respect the faith and love of an older generation, especially those who have been loyal friends to their parents. So even though we may not have our own children, there is a wonderful children's and youth ministry for spiritual "aunts" and "uncles" who get involved with and pray for the young people in a church family. Indeed, while one of the costs of planting small churches is that our kids won't have a large youthwork-based social life to enjoy, one of the benefits of being in a small church plant is to have impressively committed Christians as spiritual aunts and uncles in the lives of our children. They can often discuss more openly with our teenagers the things that our teenagers don't want to discuss with us.

So let's not fail to testify to the children and young people in our lives; let's buy them children's books and Bibles for birthdays, pay for them to go on Christian camps to find a Christian peer group in the summer, and above all, let's pray for God's blessing on them.

JOSEPH

By faith Joseph, when his end was near, spoke about the exodus of the Israelites from Egypt and gave instructions concerning the burial of his bones.

(Hebrews 11 v 22)

Joseph, of *Joseph and the Amazing Technicolor Dreamcoat* fame, was despised and sold by his brothers but lifted up by God to become prime minister of Egypt, to save God's people in a time of terrible famine. This foreshadowed Jesus, who would be despised and crucified by the people of Israel but raised and enthroned by God to be the Saviour of his people. When Joseph was old and about to die, he gathered his brothers and by faith declared, "I am about to die. But God will surely come to your aid and take you up out of this land to the land he promised on oath to Abraham, Isaac and Jacob" and then "You must carry my bones up from this place" (Genesis 50 v 24-25), because he wanted his body to be buried in God's kingdom.

Presumably, by this gesture, he wanted to demonstrate to his family his confidence in God's gospel. He asked not to be buried in a grand pyramid tomb of the sort from which the Egyptian kings hoped to be raised to an afterlife with all their wealth. His hope for eternity was in God's gospel promise. This was presumably more than sentimental; like his forebears, he probably realised that the promised land of Canaan was an earthly pledge of God's heavenly kingdom paradise, into which God would bring his people by resurrection. For when Jesus debated with the Sadducees, who didn't believe in the resurrection (presumably that's why they were "sad, you see"), Jesus said something amazing:

Are you not in error because you do not know the Scriptures or the power of God? ... Now about the dead rising—have you not read in the Book of Moses, in the account of the burning bush, how God said to him, "I am the God of Abraham, the God of Isaac and the God of Jacob"? He is not the God of the dead, but of the living. You are badly mistaken!"

(Mark 12 v 24, 26-27)

In other words, the Lord is their God because they are alive and living with him! So when the Lord introduced himself to Jacob in Genesis 28, he said, "I *am* the LORD, the God of your father Abraham and the God of Isaac" (v 13), not "I *was* the God of your father Abraham", even though Abraham was already dead! For God never abandons his people. His relationships with all his people, adopted into Christ by faith, are always current and in the present tense. He keeps the spirits of his dead people close to him (Luke 16 v 22) until one day, when Christ returns to judge and renew all things, God will give new bodies to both his dead and living people so that they can enjoy new life in his paradise kingdom.

Those who have not believed will tragically be left out in an eternity without God, which Jesus described as like living for ever infested with worms and burning in flames. This is not because God is a torturer but because he is like a "consuming fire" in his holiness (Hebrews 12 v 29). So arriving in his presence without being clothed in the righteous life of Christ is like arriving naked on the fiery surface of the sun. To some extent, the patriarchs realised this. Joseph wanted his family and descendants to live by faith in God.

So what are our aspirations and ambitions for ourselves, our kids and our church families? Here are three life-changing necessary implications.

a) Our ambition and aspiration will supremely be for our own family and our church members to be saved through faith in the gospel. Far more important than school grades or university degrees or careers, the thing we will pray for and work towards is our children and grandchildren becoming Christians. We will aspire to give them not just music lessons but the gospel. We will aspire to serve in our church ministry to children and youth in any way we can, perhaps leading or assisting in a church Scripture class, or financing children's workers or a fund to enable kids—including less privileged ones—to get to a good Christian summer camp. (Ask your pastor or church youth leader for their recommendation of a good camp.) Such summer camps have proved enormously important in the lives of so many children (and in the training of students and young workers in gospel ministry). Above all we will make the faith of our children and grandchildren, and the children of our church family, the focus of our sustained and regular prayer commitment. For we care much more about them being in heaven than being at university.

b) We will do what we can to enable more kids to hear about Jesus. If we are blessed with marriage and the capacity to have our own children, our supreme aim will not be our own satisfaction but having children who will glorify God through bringing other people to know him too. As the creation mandate to go forth and multiply is now fulfilled in the Great Commission of our Lord Jesus—to "go and make disciples of all nations" (Matthew 28 v 19)—we will commit ourselves wherever we can to gospel ministries for children, youth and students: the next generation. Perhaps we can help fund Bibles and missions for schools; or work to reduce abortion rates so that the unborn can hear the gospel; or we may explore the huge commitment of fostering or adopting children so that, God-willing, they can not only experience the joy of a loving and stable home on earth but supremely experience the joy of God's stable, loving home in heaven.

c) We will encourage our kids and young people to explore avenues to maximise their gospel ministries. Instead of enabling their indulgence in worldly priorities that only spur them to pursue the salary of a lawyer or the status of a doctor or the fulfilment of a school teacher, we will encourage them to lead a small group or outreach course, or explore overseas mission or ministry training roles with a local church, not least by celebrating their evangelistic efforts as much as their promotions and purchases. For when they stand before Jesus one day, what they earn or own will be of absolutely no value. So let's encourage and enable our children and youth and students, as the people God has made them to be, to maximise their gospel ministries.

The wonderful UK-based *Faith in Kids* ministry (faithinkids.org) reckons that 60% of Christians in the UK became Christians before they were 18—and a further 10% while they were at university. It remains obvious that, like the patriarchs, people of faith in God's gospel should pray for and commend the gospel to kids and young people.

At the beginning of the book of Judges there is an incredibly sad observation made about the time when the generation who had been led by the great leader Joshua into the promised land finally died:

> After that whole generation had been gathered to their ancestors, another generation grew up who knew neither the LORD nor what he had done for Israel. Then the Israelites did evil in the eyes of the LORD and served the Baals.   (Judges 2 v 10-11)

What was their problem? There had been no investment in children's ministry.

Let us follow the examples of Isaac, Jacob and Joseph—who acted by faith given by God—in this: may our aspirations and prayers for the next generation be gospel aspirations and gospel prayers—by faith.

7. COURAGEOUS

By faith Moses' parents disobeyed an immoral law

By faith Moses' parents hid him for three months after
he was born, because they saw he was no ordinary child,
and they were not afraid of the king's edict.

(Hebrews 11 v 23)

Anne Askew (1521-1546) was burned alive in London for her faith in the word of God. She was aged just 26. She had lived in Lincoln and was married to a Roman Catholic. But as she studied her Bible, she could no longer accept the Roman Catholic teaching of the Mass—that in the Lord's Supper the bread and wine turn into the spiritual body and blood of Jesus to be re-presented as a sacrifice for our sins by a priest on an altar. She realised that the Bible teaches that Christ has died once and for all on the cross for all our sins and is now risen and reigning in heaven. She began to welcome the "Protestant" faith of the Bible instead of the doctrines of Rome, which were compulsory by law at the time under the brutal reign of "Bloody" Queen Mary. Anne's cruel husband became ashamed of her new faith and threw her out. We don't know what happened to her two children. She came to London to meet with other Christians and became a "gospeller" or street evangelist.

In 1545 she was arrested and sent back to Lincoln. But she escaped and went back south to continue proclaiming the good news on the streets of London. In 1546 she was arrested and sent for a month to the Tower of London, where she was tortured for two days on the rack but refused to name other evangelists, despite her elbows, shoulders, hips, knees and ankles all being dislocated. A month later, on 16th July, too broken to walk, she was carried to Smithfield Market to be burned alive with three other "reformers"; though, because of her refusal to name other evangelists, Anne was burned slowly over an hour.

While chained to the stake in the flames, as Bishop Shaxton preached at her and the other martyrs to recant their faith and return to Catholicism, she courageously proclaimed her agreement at anything biblical and her disapproval of anything unbiblical, calling out "There he misses and speaks without the book"! Like the other Reformers, Anne Askew was contending for the truth of the Bible, for the salvation of many to the glory of God. But from where did she find such amazing courage to defy the authorities and endure such cruel persecution for the gospel?

By faith.

Hebrews was written for believers who were once zealous for Christ. But they were now weary of the cost of following

Jesus. The author recalls how they had "endured in a great conflict full of suffering" and were "publicly exposed to insult and persecution". He says, "You suffered along with those in prison and joyfully accepted the confiscation of your property, because you knew that you yourselves had better and lasting possessions" (10 v 32-35). Because of their faith in Christ—their confident hope of life with God in the new creation promised by the gospel—they had endured persecution by the Roman state authorities. But the hostility was taking its toll. After so much repression they were now tempted to shrink back from public loyalty to Christ. They were drawing back from any possibility of suffering like Anne Askew.

But without enduring faith in the gospel of Christ, no one can be saved. The writer to the Hebrews has been urging them to keep going. "Do not throw away your confidence; it will be richly rewarded," he says. "You need to persevere so that when you have done the will of God, you will receive what he has promised" (10 v 35). For God had previously warned, "I take no pleasure in the one who shrinks back" (10 v 38).

GOD PRESERVES US BY ENCOURAGING AND WARNING US TO PERSEVERE

At this point, we may feel a bit confused. Paul wrote, "For it is by grace you have been saved, through faith—and this is not from yourselves, it is the gift of God—not by works, so that no one can boast" (Ephesians 2 v 8). Since salvation is a *gift*, received through the faith which God creates in us through the gospel, how can these Christians be in danger of losing their reward? After all, Jesus reassured all who come to him with a double-lock security:

> I give them eternal life, and they shall never perish; no one will snatch them out of my hand. My Father, who has given them to me, is greater than all; no one can snatch them out of my Father's hand. I and the Father are one.   (John 10 v 28-30)

So how can these Christians, who have been through so much for Christ, possibly be in danger of losing their salvation? Are we in the same danger?

In answering this question we must begin by underlining Jesus' promise that real Christians cannot be snatched away from Christ or lose their salvation, for multiple reasons. It is absolutely impossible for someone chosen and predestined by God the Father from before the creation of the world, whose sins have been paid for on the cross by God the Son, who has been reborn ("regenerated") and indwelt by God the Holy Spirit as a deposit and guarantee of heaven, whose name has been written in the book of life, to then lose their salvation. The saying is true, "Once saved, always saved". Jesus is quite explicit on this point: "And this is the will of him who sent me, that I shall lose none of all those he has given me" (John 6 v 39). If we have come by faith to Jesus for salvation, we shall definitely be raised to glory when Christ returns, however much we fail and however weak our faith, because we are saved in Christ.

I love that illustration about different passengers boarding a plane bound for a paradise holiday. Some passengers will be well prepared and board early in an organised manner; others will arrive in a disorganised mess just as the doors are closing. Some will love flying and enjoy the flight; others will be terrified and be gripping their seats in terror. Some will listen carefully to the air crew and be kind to their fellow passengers, while others will complain about the food and be grumpy with everyone else. But the plane will take everyone to the same holiday destination irrespective of how they arrived or how they feel or behave during the flight. What kind of passenger you are doesn't threaten your arrival at the final destination. If you're on the plane, you're on your way to paradise! Being "in Christ" by faith is like that. Wherever we come from, whatever we've done, however we feel and however we behave, if we are in Christ by faith, we're on our way to heaven. Full stop.

But... how do we know if we are in Christ? How do we know if we have genuinely come to Jesus by faith? We don't need to have remarkable faith because we have a remarkable Saviour. But we do need to have faith. And various New Testament passages clarify that some people mistakenly assume they have saving faith—perhaps because they were raised in a Christian family, attended a Christian school or married a Christian. But the Bible warns about self-delusion by clarifying what real faith looks like.

For instance, the book of James clarifies that *saving faith is always active faith*: although we are saved by the good works of Christ and not our own good works, nevertheless, saving faith is always *expressed in good works*. We are not saved *by* our godliness, but we are saved *for* godliness! So if someone claims to have faith but there is no evidence of it in their behaviour, then they probably don't have saving faith.

Hebrews makes a similar point: *saving faith is always persevering faith*. When the Spirit of God creates new life in us by his word, expressed in saving faith in Christ, this new life of faith is eternal, and so such faith always perseveres to the end. Genuine faith always perseveres.

But this raises a question. Why does Hebrews keep encouraging and challenging the readers to persevere if we already know they will? Because the *way* God preserves and keeps his children living by faith is *through* the encouragements and warnings of his word! So, having decisively saved us when Christ died for us on the cross, he now involves us by giving us saving faith through the gospel and preserving this faith by encouraging and challenging us to *persevere*. Many Bible passages speak of God sovereignly sustaining us by grace through calling us to *keep going*. For example, consider carefully these verses:

> Continue to work out your salvation with fear and trembling, for it is God who works in you to will and to act in order to fulfil his good purpose.
>
> (Philippians 2 v 12-13)

So who is sustaining our saving faith—is it us or is it God? The answer is that *God* does it… *through us!* We must work at persevering, knowing that God is working through our work to preserve us. So he does save us by his grace alone, empowering our saving faith in him, by encouraging and warning us through his word.

This was the realisation of the great African theologian Augustine of Hippo (AD 354-430), and one which would eventually flourish in the Reformation discovery of salvation by grace alone (against his own faulty doctrines of the church). But this doctrine enraged his opponent, Pelagius, the British monk who championed human free will and self-determination. Augustine prayed to God, "Command what you wish, but give what you command"—meaning that he knew he could not obey God unless God freed him from his personal addiction to sin, especially his lust. He knew from personal experience that our wills are not free but enslaved by sin. And so our faith cannot persevere unless God empowers it. We will give up our faith unless God strengthens it—which he does by his Holy Spirit through his word.

GOD TREATS US AS HIS CHILDREN, NOT HIS ROBOTS

The reason God preserves us through our perseverance is that he did not create or redeem us to be robots programmed to serve him. He has adopted us as children to know and love and enjoy him. So imagine a dad teaching his little son or daughter to play cricket or baseball. Holding his child's hands as they hold the plastic bat, the dad says, "Now don't rush, wait for the ball, keep watching the ball, and now hit it like this. Well done, you smashed it!" as the ball is launched into the distance. Dad has supplied all the power and timing and skill required, but he has involved his child to teach them how to do what he can do! That's how God teaches us to live by faith—warning and encouraging us to do what he is empowering us to do—to live by faith... by his grace alone.

That's why the writer to the Hebrews both warns and encourages his readers, genuinely urging them to persevere and, at the same time, genuinely confident that they will. For example, in 10 v 36 the writer challenges them saying, "You need to persevere" and warns them in 10 v 38 that God has said, "I take no pleasure in the one who shrinks back". But then the writer reassures them in 10 v 39: "But we do not belong to those who shrink back and are destroyed, but to those who have faith and are saved". Through warnings and encouragements to persevere, God preserves his people—by his Spirit speaking through his word to sustain their faith.

Now, in chapter 11, he's encouraging his readers by recounting how God has enabled Old Testament believers—not just great heroes of faith but almost anyone you can remember—to live by faith in God's gospel promise. Having spoken of the ancients and the patriarchs, he is now about to speak of the great prophet Moses, who gave up life as a prince of Egypt to join the Hebrew slaves in their future promised by God.

But before speaking of Moses, he sees the opportunity to address a worrying dilemma facing his persecuted readers—whether to defy the law of the Roman Empire. They needed the courage of their convictions to be strengthened.

Hebrews 12 v 4 says, "You have not yet resisted to the point of shedding your blood". So it is likely that the persecution being referred to is not the horrific repressions under Nero and Domitian (in the 60s and 90s of the first century) when many Christians were cruelly martyred. It is more probably the earlier persecution under Claudius in AD 49 when, according to the historian Suetonius, the Jews were expelled from Rome because of riots in the Jewish community concerning *Chrestus* (almost certainly Christ). Christianity had been declared "an illegal superstition" by the Roman Senate but had been tolerated under Emperor Tiberius (who hoped it would weaken troublesome Jewish nationalism). But now the Christians were suffering eviction from their homes, economic oppression and even imprisonment. It must have been very worrying for the Christian readers to find their evangelism now considered illegal, as it is today for Christians living in Muslim countries such as Saudi Arabia and Yemen. Indeed, some aspects of biblical faith—such as convictions about gender being God-given and sexual activity being reserved for marriage between a man and a woman—may soon face legal sanction in Western countries such as the UK.

So the writer takes the opportunity to mention two little-known believers who, by their faith in God, defied an unbiblical law with great courage: namely, Moses' parents.

BY FAITH MOSES' PARENTS DEFIED AN IMMORAL LAW

By faith Moses' parents hid him for three months after he was born, because they saw he was no ordinary child, and they were not afraid of the king's edict.   (Hebrews 11 v 23)

By their faith, Moses' parents, Amram and Jochebed, recognised that Moses was "no ordinary child" (literally "a beautiful child", as Stephen puts it in Acts 7 v 20). This doesn't mean he had dreamy eyes or was a music or chess prodigy, but that he was beautiful to God, meaning precious in the Lord's plans for the redemption of Israel from slavery. Of course, every parent wants to protect their baby. But when Pharaoh became worried that the Hebrew slaves were becoming so numerous as to be threatening, and so commanded that all Hebrew baby boys under two must be killed, anyone defying this law could expect to be executed. Moses' parents had his older sister Miriam to worry about as well as each other. The law of the land required them to surrender their baby and grieve quietly. But this verse says it was their *faith* in God which empowered their courage to defy Pharaoh's edict and break the law. They hid the baby Moses for three months and then placed him in a basket, to be found and adopted by Pharaoh's daughter, because, by faith, "they were not afraid of the king's edict".

Faith in God has empowered many in biblical and church history to ethical civil disobedience. This is becoming an important issue in Western nations, which have recently become polarised over divisive political and ethical issues such as election or referendum results, concerns about climate change championed by campaigners like David Attenborough, issues of systemic racism and injustice raised by the shocking murder of George Floyd in May 2020, and appalling abortion rates. Christians want to know if they can or should protest, march, defy immoral laws or engage in civil disobedience if the law requires us to live contrary to the Bible.

The apostle Paul writes, "Let everyone be subject to the governing authorities" (Romans 13 v 1). When he speaks of "governing authorities", he surely includes national and local governments who make our laws and the courts and police who enforce them. It is sobering to remember that Paul was living in the Roman Empire, which was often ruled by insanely violent Caesars, and he was repeatedly arrested, imprisoned and beaten by repressive local authorities provoked by Jewish religious extremism. But Paul insists that Christians must be good citizens and not troublemakers. Christians are to be *spiritually* but not politically revolutionary. So he says, "Let everyone be subject" to government directions.

As God is three Persons in loving community—Father, Son and Holy Spirit, equal in status but ordered in roles of loving authority and submission—so in all our human relationships there is authority and submission between people who are equal in dignity but have different roles. So children should submit to parents, employees to employers, church members to elders, wives to husbands, and all of us to our governing authorities. Paul explains, "There is no authority except that which God has established ... whoever rebels against the authority is rebelling against what God has instituted, and those who do so will bring judgment upon themselves".

God is in control of the outcomes of elections and wars and social movements, for "the Most High is sovereign over all kingdoms on earth and gives them to anyone he wishes" (Daniel 4 v 25). Indeed, he may judge a nation of sinners by giving us up to a godless government and its reckless policies to expose our need of his word and the governance of his Son. Or he may appoint a repressive government to test and strengthen our faith.

Nevertheless, Paul was willing to use the legal rights granted to him by Roman law to prevent injustice. So, for example, he appealed against his arrest in Acts 22, not least to protect the reputation of other Christians.

And the Bible does place very important limits upon our submission to state authorities, of which the first example here is what is referred to in Hebrews 11 v 23:

- If obedience would involve *immorality*: e.g. the Hebrew midwives who would not obey Pharaoh's command to kill baby boys (Exodus 2), just as Christian doctors will avoid colluding with abortion

- If obedience would involve *abuse of power*: e.g. as when Nathan the prophet confronted David's adultery with Bathsheba and the murder of her husband, just as Christians today, while "turning the other cheek" to personal hurts, will protest against and challenge rulers or bosses or pastors who abuse their power

- If obedience would involve *idolatry*: e.g. Shadrach, Meshak and Abednego, who would not obey the king's command to bow in worship of his golden statue (Daniel 2), just as Christians today will not participate in multi-faith worship

- If obedience would involve *silencing the gospel*: e.g. as when the apostles told the ruling Sanhedrin council that they must obey God and not cease evangelism, just as Christians today cannot agree to stop speaking about Jesus with gentleness and respect.

The late great British preacher and author John Stott summarised these limits like this: "If the state commands what God forbids or forbids what God commands, then our plain Christian duty is to resist, not to submit—to disobey the state in order to obey God" (*Issues Facing Christians Today*); or, as the apostle Peter puts it, "We must obey God rather than man" (Acts 5). There are countless issues that the state is free to determine, and we must accept those policies even if we disagree with them. But if the state is contradicting God's word, we are bound to disobey because all rulers and people are subject to God.

This is what Moses' parents courageously did by faith, despite the danger from Pharaoh. (Indeed, their faith points forward to that of Joseph and Mary, Jesus' parents, who rescued the baby Jesus from Herod by fleeing the country and taking him down to Egypt.)

By our faith in God's word, Christians will want to use any rights we enjoy from our government to protest against all kinds of unrighteousness and injustice, such as marching to protest at ecological irresponsibility, racial injustice and abortion. And, where a government or employer is blatantly guilty of promoting serious immorality, abuse of power, idolatry or suppression of the gospel, we have to confront them and defy their immoral commands—without ever resorting to wanton vandalism or terrorism—and accept the penal consequences.

By faith, Moses' parents risked their lives to disobey Pharaoh to further God's salvation, as by faith Elijah risked his life to condemn Ahab and challenge Jezebel; as by faith Daniel disobeyed Darius and was thrown to the lions; as by faith John the Baptist condemned Herod's marriage to his brother's wife and was executed; as by faith Latimer and Ridley refused to say that Christ is on the table in the Lord's Supper and were burned alive; as by faith the "Confessing Church" leaders in 1930s Germany, like Barth, Bonhoeffer and Niemoller, rejected any notion that the church could be directed by the state or Fuhrer instead of the word of God; as by faith in December 2018 the prominent evangelical Chinese pastor, Wang Yi, criticised the Chinese government for requiring its citizens to engage in the "Caesar-worship" of President Xi Jinping as if he were a god, before being arrested together with 100 members of his Early Rain Covenant Church, since when he has not been seen .

By faith, we can, like Moses' parents and so many Christians since, trust God enough and care for people enough to challenge and, if necessary, defy laws that impose immorality, abuse power, require idolatry, or silence the gospel, because by faith our conviction is that Jesus is Lord over presidents and parliaments and prelates, and so we are not afraid of powerful human authorities. And by faith in his word, God's Spirit will give us the courage we need to defy wicked employers and governments and denominations without being afraid of the consequences—because we are now living by faith in the King of kings, and Lord of lords!

8. SELF-DENYING

By faith Moses chose mistreatment instead of pleasure

By faith Moses, when he had grown up, refused to be known as the son of Pharaoh's daughter. He chose to be ill-treated along with the people of God rather than to enjoy the fleeting pleasures of sin. He regarded disgrace for the sake of Christ as of greater value than the treasures of Egypt, because he was looking ahead to his reward. By faith he left Egypt, not fearing the king's anger; he persevered because he saw him who is invisible. By faith he kept the Passover and the application of blood, so that the destroyer of the firstborn would not touch the firstborn of Israel.

(Hebrews 11 v 24-28)

Billy Vunipola, the Saracens and England rugby player, has got himself into hot water for his Christian faith recently. In 2019, in support of Israel Folau, another Australian Christian rugby player who was sacked by Rugby Australia for inflammatory comments about homosexuals, Billy posted, "Man was made for women to procreate, that was the goal no?" and was promptly given formal warnings by the English Rugby Football Union and Saracens. Then in 2020, he was one of a number of players who chose to stand against racism but not by "taking a knee" in support of Black Lives Matter. He has explained, "What I saw in terms of the Black Lives Matter movement was not aligned with what I believe in ... Even though I am a person of colour, I'm still more a person of, I guess, Jesus." Reflecting on his support for Folau, he explained, "I didn't sleep for two or three days when I saw the post because something inside me was saying, 'Do you actually believe in Jesus Christ or do you not? ... Am I going to put myself in a position where people dislike me and ridicule me?' I didn't enjoy being ridiculed. But what I did find comforting is that I stood up for my faith and didn't fall by the wayside" (*The Daily Telegraph*, 20 August 2020). Perhaps Billy was clumsy in his choice of words (Israel Folau certainly was), but he was clearly trying to stand up for the teachings of Jesus. The writer of Hebrews 11 would have been proud of Billy, as we should be too.

Faith in Christ will always be costly. It's costly in terms of leaving sinful pleasures behind; and it's costly in terms of the hostility we're likely to face. Jesus talked about the cost of Christian faith when he said, "Whoever wants to be my disciple must *deny themselves* and *take up their cross* and *follow me*" (Mark 8 v 34).

a) Deny themselves

This means neglecting our own needs for the sake of others. This isn't "asceticism": trying to impress God with pointless hardship, like the famous 5th-century monk Simeon Stylites, who sold his possessions to go and live alone in the Syrian desert to pray on top of a stone pillar for 37 years. Actually, the apostle Paul says that forbidding the grateful enjoyment of God's good gifts, such as marriage and food, is demonic (1 Timothy 4 v 1-4) because it denies our heavenly Father's kindness in lovingly providing for us. As I said earlier, Jesus wasn't a *masochist*, who went to the cross because he likes pain, but a *Saviour*, who went to the cross because it was the only way to save sinners. Like Jesus, we can enjoy the blessings our Father provides, but we will make costly sacrifices for the salvation of sinners. To "deny yourself" means putting others before yourself, especially for their salvation.

b) Take up their cross

This means accepting suffering for the salvation of others. Jesus is saying *we must carry a cross of suffering on earth if we want to wear a crown of victory in heaven*. Notice that Jesus says "take up", meaning "pick it up"! He will not force us to do so. He calls us to voluntarily accept suffering for the salvation of others. And notice that he says his followers must take up "their cross". It will not be *Jesus'* cross, on which he alone suffered for our sins; it will not be *anyone else's* cross, so we mustn't compare or compete; it will not be the cross *we choose* but the one chosen for us by our loving heavenly Father. It will be the cost of contributing what we can, as the people we are, towards the mission of making disciples of all nations for him. And notice Jesus speaks of our "cross"—not the sicknesses and hardships of life but the specific costs of supporting the proclamation of Christ crucified.

I've been thrilled to see God empowering ordinary people, across the churches of our Co-Mission church-planting and strengthening network in London, to make all sorts of sacrifice for his gospel. Some have moved house to an area they didn't want to live in to help start ("plant") a new church, and others have stayed where they live instead of pursuing more space for their family, in order to support their existing church; some have given up well-paid careers to train for gospel ministry, while others have stayed in demanding careers to finance them; others have pounded the streets from door to door, inviting people to come and hear about Jesus or given up countless evenings organising outreach to foreign students, to the elderly, to those in prison or to sex-workers.

c) Follow me

This means learning from Jesus how to live by faith in a life of evangelistic holiness for our Father. In Mark 8, Jesus commends the long-term wisdom of this lifestyle with some simple commercially derived principles. He says:

- think about *savings* (v 35): "For whoever wants to save their life will lose it, but whoever loses their life for me and for the gospel will save it." We recognise the wisdom of saving for the future, for a wedding or for retirement. Jesus says that if we try to save our lives for ourselves, we'll lose life with God, but if we give up our life to serve his mission to save sinners, God will save us for life with him in heaven.

- think about *investments* (v 36): "What good is it for someone to gain the whole world, yet forfeit their soul?" We recognise the wisdom of investing wisely, perhaps in a property that grows in value. But there's no point in investing in becoming as rich as British billionaire and chairman of Virgin Group, Sir Richard Branson, if we have nothing invested in our relationship with God for eternity! Better to invest in supporting God's mission now if we want to live with him then.

- think about *currency* (v 37): "What can anyone give in exchange for their soul?" We all recognise the wisdom of having the right currency abroad—a huge wad of £100 notes is useless in France. So if the currency that works in heaven is not success and popularity but self-sacrificially following Jesus, then follow him.

- think about *loyalty* (v 38): "If anyone is ashamed of me and my words in this adulterous and sinful generation, the Son of Man will be ashamed of them when he comes in his Father's glory with the holy angels." We all recognise the wisdom of loyalty to the boss. Jesus reminds us that he's coming back to resurrect everyone to face his judgment. If we've been loyal to him and his gospel—believing, proclaiming and contending for Christ and his teaching, even if it is politically incorrect—he'll be loyal to us.

This way of the cross, which Jesus calls us to follow, is a lifestyle of self-denial, modelled in the life of Moses, who surrendered his life of luxury as a prince of Egypt to live by faith among God's suffering people.

Moses was probably the greatest hero of Jewish history, commended by God in Hebrews 3 v 2 as "faithful in all God's house". We may know a bit about him from films such as *The Prince of Egypt*, but the New Testament writers assume that we'll have read his amazing story in the book of Exodus. God used him to rescue Israel from slavery—an event that he planned to show what Jesus has done for us.

Moses was famously raised in the opulence and power of the court of the Egyptian pharaohs. But then, as an adult, he made three critical decisions in which he chose to live by faith in God's gospel promise; each of these is an inspiring example for readers of Hebrews then and now.

BY FAITH MOSES REFUSED A LIFE OF PRIVILEGE

By faith Moses, when he had grown up, refused to be known as the son of Pharaoh's daughter.

(Hebrews 11 v 24)

Moses was brought up by Pharaoh's daughter as her own son. This was probably in the reign of a pharaoh of the nineteenth dynasty (c.1300 BC). Moses was "educated in all the wisdom of the Egyptians and was powerful in speech and action" (Acts 7 v 21-22); he was an impressive and privileged prince of the Egyptian Empire. As a boy he was probably encouraged to expect high office in the empire. But Moses chose a humbler route.

When Moses was forty, "he decided to visit his own people, the Israelites. He saw one of them being ill-treated by an Egyptian, so he went to his defence and avenged him by killing the Egyptian" (Acts 7 v 23). In starting to visit the Israelites, Moses was clearly beginning to identify with his own people, who were enslaved, rather than with Pharaoh's household and the Egyptian ruling class. Hebrews concludes that he "refused to be known as the son of Pharaoh's daughter". He was willing to surrender the status and comforts of royalty for the contempt and privations of God's people. This surrender of status was "by faith", because we know that Moses had already heard of his commission from God to be the deliverer of Israel, since Acts 7 v 25 tells us, "Moses thought that his own people would realise that God was using him to rescue them".

Christians are all commissioned by Jesus to "make disciples of all nations" (Matthew 28 v 19), and we shall need to surrender ourselves, like Moses, to this calling "by faith". Moses' decision reflects the same sort of priority as that shown by legendary English missionary C.T. Studd (1860-1931). Having captained the Cambridge University and England cricket teams, a glittering career awaited him. But Studd abandoned his celebrity status to labour as a missionary in China, then in India and later in

Africa. Like Moses, he surrendered his status and power for the sake of the gospel.

Even if we are nothing like an Egyptian prince, by faith we can do the same as Moses. Many have sacrificed their reputation in a secular company by trying to evangelise their colleagues. Many have been bypassed at work because they endeavour to get home to pray with their kids before bedtime or lead a weekly youth outreach rather than curry favour by socialising with bosses. Many have given up prestigious careers to become gospel workers. By faith in the gospel, we too can surrender our worldly status. Moses was making a deliberate choice:

He chose to be ill-treated along with the people of God rather than to enjoy the fleeting pleasures of sin.
(Hebrews 11 v 25)

The writer doesn't clarify what pleasures of sin he is referring to, but the hedonism of the pagan Egyptian court was legendary. Of course, political power and high rank can be used for good—as Joseph had shown when he was elevated to become prime minister in Egypt four centuries earlier. And the work of William Wilberforce and others in Britain and the British Parliament to abolish the slave trade is eloquent testimony to what can sometimes be done by God through Christians of high rank (even if they were blind to other evils of colonial exploitation from which they benefitted).

For Moses to reject God's mission in order to keep control of his life and enjoy some selfish pleasures (which never satisfy our soul) would have been foolishly short-sighted. A few highs in the harem are never worth an eternity in the horrors of hell. The same is true today. Furthermore Christians sometimes have an overly rosy view of what sin is like. Many years ago when I was a student, as a Christian who rather self-pityingly resented having to avoid the hedonistic lifestyle of my friends, I sheepishly asked the biggest playboy in my year what it was like having so many sexual partners. His answer surprised me. "Richard, it's awful. I wake up next to someone whose name I can't remember and hate myself." Maybe sin is emptier than it looks.

Instead, Moses "chose to be ill-treated along with the people of God". For Moses, this was to choose the contempt, poverty and slavery of the Hebrews. It was not that Moses wanted ill-treatment but that he wanted to join the people of God. So why would a prince of Egypt ditch the dream life to join a despised and oppressed people?

> He regarded disgrace for the sake of Christ as of
> greater value than the treasures of Egypt, because he
> was looking ahead to his reward.   (Hebrews 11 v 26)

To abandon the opulent comforts of civilised life in his own palatial home for the hovels of the slaves and his exile in Midian must have looked like madness. But Moses preferred this disgrace "for the sake of Christ". This certainly doesn't mean that Moses knew Christ as we now know him. (The incarnation of Christ, the sending of the Holy Spirit at Pentecost, and the writing of the New Testament—the God-given means by which Christians have come to know Christ—were not available to Old Testament believers.) It could mean that in choosing to join the Israelites, it was theologically as if Moses chose Christ. I wonder if the best interpretation is much simpler. The word "Christ" means "anointed" or "chosen". When Hebrews 11 says that Moses preferred "disgrace for the sake of Christ" (the *chosen*), it seems more likely that the author means the *chosen* people of Israel. Moses realised it was more valuable in the long run to suffer disgrace for God's people on their way to an eternity with God than to enjoy the pleasures and treasures of Pharaoh for one short lifetime. Of course, the pharaohs tried to take their immense fortunes into the afterlife by having treasures interred with them in the burial chambers of their pyramids. But grave robbers and archaeologists got the lot. Moses realised that the future blessings of God's chosen people will last for ever.

One of the finest examples of this long-term perspective of faith is provided by Eric Liddell, the "Flying Scotsman" of *Chariots of Fire* fame. He played international rugby for Scotland but is more famous for his sprinting. He won multiple national championships, and in 1924 in Paris, he won the Olympic 400m gold medal. But he is most admired for three extraordinary decisions that reflected his deep surrender to our heavenly Father's will.

The first was his bold decision not to run in his preferred 100m race at the Olympics, because the heats were to be run on a Sunday. It was his settled conviction that Sunday should be kept special for the Lord. He was

accused of being a traitor to his country, but as Harold
Abrahams, whom he'd earlier beaten, was winning the
gold medal, Eric was preaching in a church in Paris. He
desired God's approval more than an Olympic medal.

After winning the gold in his weaker event of 400m
in a world-record time, the world lay at his feet. But now
came his second decision surrendered to the will of God.
Eric Liddell enrolled at Bible college and then announced
that he was going to Tientsin, in China, as a missionary,
aged 23, to make disciples of all nations for Jesus.

Ordained in 1932, married in 1933 and soon with
three daughters, he made a third sacrificial decision in
1937. With the support of his wife but despite severe
criticism, he responded to desperate pleas for help from
missionaries in the war-torn country region of Siaochang
and began leaving his family for long periods to help
with gospel work there. In 1942 he was trapped by the
oncoming Japanese armies and bundled off with other
Europeans to the prison compound of Weihsien. There,
separated from his family, he dedicated himself to the
welfare of others and commending the gospel, before
dying of a brain tumour in 1945.

All of Scotland mourned this man who had cared
more for God's glory than his own. The guiding principle
of his life, and the last word on his lips as he died, was
"surrender". Like Moses, Eric surrendered himself to
God's priorities, by faith.

BY FAITH MOSES LEFT EGYPT

> By faith he left Egypt, not fearing the king's anger;
> he persevered because he saw him who is invisible.
>
> (Hebrews 11 v 27)

When Moses grew up, he killed an Egyptian whom he had found mistreating a Hebrew slave (Exodus 2; Acts 7). When Pharaoh then tried to kill him, Moses fled to live in Midian for forty years until the Lord called to him from a burning bush and sent him back to Egypt to redeem his people.

This verse explicitly says that Moses was not afraid of the king. It could be that this refers to later, when Moses left Egypt in the great exodus of Israel, but it would be strange to speak of the exodus before speaking of the Passover in the next verse. More likely this refers to Moses not being afraid of Pharaoh when he left for Midian, although we know he was afraid when he discovered that his fellow Hebrews knew what he'd done (presumably he feared that he had already failed God's call to lead his people). The writer of Hebrews 11 is saying that Moses' faith in the Lord removed his fear of the king and made him willing to leave Egypt without Pharaoh's permission.

He then lived in Midian—"he settled as a foreigner and had two sons" (Acts 7 v 29)—waiting by faith for forty more years until the Lord finally called him back to liberate his people. Having been told he'd be Israel's deliverer, Moses didn't try to invent his own way of doing it or to run away from it. With patient faith, he waited for God's direction. Being a Christian often involves faithfully waiting for opportunities to serve—often by accepting some training that we will need in order to do the ministry well.

Why was Moses so patient? He waited many years in Egypt and then forty years in Midian for the Lord to do what he had promised. Why? Because "he saw him who is invisible"—not visibly (in the flames of the fiery bush) but spiritually by his faith. Moses was convinced that the Lord, who is spirit and invisible, is real! This confidence in the reality of God removed his fear and helped him persevere. It's striking that the apostle Peter likewise tells us:

> Do not fear their threats; do not be frightened.
> But in your hearts revere Christ as Lord. Always be
> prepared to give an answer to everyone who asks
> you to give the reason for the hope that you have.
> But do this with gentleness and respect, keeping a
> clear conscience, so that those who speak maliciously
> against your good behaviour in Christ may be
> ashamed of their slander.   (1 Peter 3 v 14-16)

Being ready to give a reason for the hope that we have depends first on not being frightened, because we know by faith that Christ is Lord over every situation and every person, including us!

Faith empowers us, as it did Moses, to leave the pleasures and treasures of this world behind to patiently wait for the rewards of heaven. If our eternal life were like a rope that stretches a million times around the world, then our life on this planet would be less than the first centimetre of that rope. How absurd to resent the costs of that one centimetre of life (which, despite the hardships, is enriched by the priceless joy of knowing God) and then lose the pleasure of millions of kilometres of joy in eternity?

And then, climactically in the life of this former prince of Egypt...

BY FAITH MOSES KEPT THE PASSOVER

By faith he kept the Passover and the application of blood, so that the destroyer of the firstborn would not touch the firstborn of Israel. (Hebrews 11 v 28)

Moses believed the Lord's warning of a terrible judgment to come upon the firstborn sons of Egypt because of their idolatry and cruelty and stubborn refusal to let his oppressed people leave. He trusted the Lord's strange instructions about killing a lamb or goat and smearing its blood over the doorposts. By this faith he led the Israelites to obey the Passover instructions (Exodus 12). Each family had to keep a flawless young lamb or goat for a few days to identify with it. Then, on the night the Lord sent judgment upon Egypt, any Hebrew family who had painted the blood of sacrifice on the doorposts of their home was spared his wrath. The Lord was satisfied that death had occurred, and so the Lord "passed over" that home.

Of course, the Passover pointed forward to the death of Jesus, slaughtered in our place on the cross to satisfy God so that his judgment will pass over us.

Have you ever actually asked God to forgive you because of the death of Jesus? If you are in any doubt about this, why not pray this prayer...

Almighty God, please accept the blood of Jesus shed for my sins, and forgive me; help me to live by faith in Jesus—to leave the pleasures of sin behind, to deny myself, to take up my cross and to follow Jesus from now on, for I am looking forward to the eternal joy of being with you and your people in heaven for ever. Amen.

If you have prayed this prayer from your heart, you will be in heaven with Moses and all who live by self-denying faith in the gospel. You will find it helpful to tell a Christian friend and make contact with a Bible-teaching church near you so they can suggest some next steps.

But if you are reluctant to accept the death of Jesus for you and leave your sin behind, please beware. Apparently, catching monkeys is easy! You just put apples coated in syrup into cans or bottles, with openings only slightly larger than the apples, which are then tethered to the ground. When a monkey puts a hand into the bottle or can and closes it around the fruit, it can't then remove its hand while holding on to the apple. Indeed, rather than let go of its delicious prize, the monkey will allow itself to be easily captured, caught by its greed. Tragically, some people are like that: unable to let go of the pleasures of sin.

If you know someone like that, ask God to create in them the self-denying faith of Moses, who was willing to surrender the pleasures of sin in this world to live by faith with his despised people and to gain eternal joy in heaven with God. God can empower us all to live by the self-denying faith of the former prince of Egypt.

9. EMPOWERING

By faith we can accomplish great things

By faith the people passed through the Red Sea as on dry land; but when the Egyptians tried to do so, they were drowned.

By faith the walls of Jericho fell, after the army had marched around them for seven days.

By faith the prostitute Rahab, because she welcomed the spies, was not killed with those who were disobedient.

And what more shall I say? I do not have time to tell about Gideon, Barak, Samson and Jephthah, about David and Samuel and the prophets, who through faith conquered kingdoms, administered justice, and gained what was promised; who shut the mouths of lions, quenched the fury of the flames, and escaped the edge of the sword; whose weakness was turned to strength; and who became powerful in battle and routed foreign armies. Women received back their dead, raised to life again.

(Hebrews 11 v 29-35)

Managing expectations is vital in any enterprise because repeated disappointment and failure to reach exaggerated expectations soon becomes demoralising. And in a world of incessant commercial marketing, we are generally suspicious of inflated spin. This is particularly nauseating in ministries that exploit vulnerable Christians with exaggerated promises of health, wealth and success. These inflated claims go against what we have seen in Hebrews about Christians regularly experiencing suffering, insult, persecution, confiscation of property and more (10 v 32-34).

In truth, Jesus himself was both victorious and victimised in his life on earth—experiencing both triumphs and tribulations. So the writer of Hebrews 11 wants to manage the expectations of his weary and demoralised readers. For if Christians are taught to expect constant success, they are likely to become cynical when they face sickness, failure and opposition. On the other hand, if Christians are taught to expect little of God but failure and suffering, they are unlikely to attempt much for God.

The writer wants to demonstrate from the Old Testament that God has empowered his people by faith in both success and suffering to persevere through achievement and opposition and to endure in both prosperity and poverty. To persevere in the Christian life, we will need to have measured expectations of living by faith.

In this chapter we will hear his examples of accomplishing great things for God by faith. In the next we will hear his examples of suffering horrendous things for God by faith.

FAITH IN GOD EMPOWERS GREAT VICTORIES

Shortly after we planted our first church in Mayfair, central London, I was shown a long letter from a church pastor I know, criticising the plant. The letter bemoaned how our new little church had the wrong sort of people in the wrong kind of building in the wrong part of town at the wrong time for planting. As I read this torrent of scepticism, I had to admit that he had a point. Almost every weakness he identified was real. There were lots of problems facing us. But after reading his critique I thought to myself, "But if we wait until everything is right, we'll never plant any church at all!" Isn't it better to have a go "by faith" in the Lord who said, *All authority belongs to me. Go and make disciples of all nations, and I will be with you* (Matthew 28 v 18-19)? I certainly like the imperfect church which is there today led by my successor (a wonderful Bible-teaching ministry bursting with life and young people at Christchurch Mayfair) a lot more than the perfect church that has never been planted.

Too often Christians and churches lack the faith in the power and goodness of God to have a go and not die wondering. There's certainly no promise in Scripture that whatever we attempt will work. But Jesus' parable of the talents or bags of gold (Matthew 25 v 14-30) is quite clear that real disciples have a go, by faith, to extend the work of his kingdom, with whatever has been entrusted to them by way of resources and opportunities. They are the people to whom Jesus will say, "Well done, good and faithful servant. You have been faithful with a few things;

I will put you in charge of many things. Come and share your master's happiness."

But the servant who is too afraid to risk failure, and does nothing for the Lord with the resources entrusted to them, is the one who hears the dreadful condemnation: "Throw that worthless servant outside, into the darkness". Their inertia has demonstrated that they have no real love for God or his mission because they are not genuinely disciples of Christ. Perhaps they just liked going to church.

Being a faithful servant of the Lord requires getting involved, as the people we are with the resources we have, in the gospel initiatives that the Lord presents to us—contributing to evangelism, church-planting and revitalisation, or cross-cultural mission by our faith in Christ. After all, when we look at the little mission teams that Jesus and his apostles had with which to plant churches, we have to conclude that God can do amazing and exciting things despite our weakness.

Those amazing things might not be big in the world's estimation. I know a group of elderly widows at a church in Manchester who decided to pray on Friday evenings for a young evangelist in their church youth group. He was astonished to discover ten years later that they had been faithfully praying for him. Twenty years later the young man, Andy, and the ministries of the Message Trust, which he leads, have been used by God to bring countless young people across Manchester to Christ. And Andy is first to tell you that it was the prayers of those elderly ladies—most of whom have now died—that were

God's power behind the success of the Message Trust ministries. Such prayer doesn't look much to the world, but it honours God our Father, who is pleased to answer such prayers and grow his kingdom.

Living by faith means having a go in furthering gospel ministry—beginning with our local church—by faith in the power of God. The author of Hebrews goes on to offer a string of inspiring examples.

IN THE EXODUS

> By faith the people passed through the Red Sea as on dry land ... By faith the walls of Jericho fell ... By faith the prostitute Rahab, because she welcomed the spies, was not killed ...   (Hebrews 11 v 29-31)

Faith in God's power gave God's people the confidence and courage they needed to do something terrifying. Since God had promised to redeem Israel, the Israelites, including their small children and frail elderly, walked across the floor of the Red Sea with the waters piled up around them.

Since God had promised Israel victory over Jericho, the Israelite forces accepted God's apparently crazy military strategy of just walking repeatedly around the city until God brought the walls crashing down.

Since God had promised Israel the land of Canaan, the prostitute Rahab in the city of Jericho believed God would do what he said and resolved to change sides to join Israel. So she welcomed the spies—and encouraged them to believe God's gospel promise, which the previous generation of spies had failed to believe (Numbers 13). This converted prostitute, who began to live by faith in the gospel, is therefore honoured as one of Jesus' own ancestors (Matthew 1 v 5).

Throughout the Exodus travels, faith in God's gospel promise brought the people many victories over terrifying opposition, just as in our own exodus journey to the promised land of the new creation, nothing can prevent us arriving in victory to receive our inheritance. We can fight the good fight of faith today against sin, the world and the devil, and be victorious by looking to God with confidence that his strength will prevail. For he has promised to get us to heaven; and we believe him.

IN CANAAN

> And what more shall I say? I do not have time to tell
> about... (Hebrews 11 v 32)

The author knows he can't keep moving so slowly through the Old Testament. So he begins to summarise long periods of history with a list of people, starting with some of the judges, kings and prophets. He leaves the impression that he could choose dozens more because he is not selecting the elite "special forces" of faith—but describing the regular rank and file. He is describing what God has always enabled his people to do, by faith.

It's encouraging to consider not only what these ancient people did but also what God continues to enable people to do by faith today. It's not helpful to think that God was only active in the dim and distant past. He is enabling people to accomplish great things for the gospel today (and to him be all the glory). In our British evangelical scene, while we dislike hubris and are cautious not to exalt people, we can be guilty of an "Eeyore" mentality, which fails to appreciate encouraging gospel success and makes most of us too depressed to attempt anything bold for God.

Some "conquered kingdoms"—like *Gideon*, who, at God's command, obediently reduced his army for fighting the vast Midianite forces to just 300 watchful men, who then routed the enemy by smashing clay pots! Do you think God can't do amazing things like that today? I hear that the church in the repressive Muslim nation of Iran now numbers more than a million people! Those who laboured for the gospel and saw little fruit for so long can now rejoice at what God has done through people of faith.

Barak is so encouraging because, although he was the general of the Israelite army, he wasn't very brave at all! When the prophet Deborah relayed the word of the Lord to him, promising victory against Sisera and the Canaanites, Barak wouldn't fight unless Deborah went with him and was only victorious when Deborah told him to fight. God can use the faith of timid people like Barak—especially when they are supported by the courageous faith of women like Deborah. In the same way, many a preacher today is empowered by God through the courageous faith of their wife or of sisters in their church.

Samson, who was gifted but not godly, was used by God, despite his great weakness for Delilah, to deliver the Israelites from the Philistines. Like Jesus, Samson was victorious supremely in his death, when he stretched out his arms to break the columns of the Philistine banqueting hall to bring the roof down on the Philistine rulers (Judges 16 v 25-30). God still does this kind of thing. Jim Elliot was just 29 when he arrived as a missionary among the people of the Auca tribe of Ecuador and, with four fellow missionaries, was speared to death in 1956. It seemed like a tragic failure. Yet Christianity.com observes, "During his life, Jim Elliot longed for more people to become missionaries. In his death, however, he probably inspired more people to go to other countries to share the love of Jesus than he ever could have in life." He famously wrote in his journal, "He is no fool who gives what he cannot keep to gain that which he cannot lose".

Jephthah, despite a tragically idiotic vow that resulted in the death of his daughter, was empowered by God to defeat the Amorites and Ammonites (Judges 11 – 12). Perhaps we've made idiotic mistakes in the past. God can still accomplish great things through people who have made terrible mistakes. I think of a Korean colleague who was once the leader of the biggest gang in Seoul and was doing all sorts of idiotic things, until Christ captured and transformed him into a wonderfully effective evangelist.

David's most famous victory was clearly foreshadowing Jesus' triumph over Satan on the cross. By his faith in God, this despised shepherd confronted the terrifying giant Goliath on behalf of Israel, and by an unlikely victory with a slingshot, he prevailed over the giant and inspired the Israelite army to victory (1 Samuel 17)! But when I consider how God has used the under-resourced

Primates Council of the GAFCON movement in recent years to resist the powerful giant that is Anglican liberalism, and unite more than 60 million Anglicans around God's word to proclaim Christ faithfully from the Scriptures to all nations, we see that God is still enabling unlikely victories today.

Samuel came before David and was a towering figure, being the last of the judges as well as the prophet of God who anointed and instructed Saul and then David as the first kings of Israel. Perhaps the prophet Samuel reminds us of the American evangelist Billy Graham, who preached the message of Christ's freedom and forgiveness around the world for more than 50 years, reaching over 200 million people in more than 185 countries. He invited hundreds of thousands of people to pray to receive Jesus Christ into their lives as Lord and Saviour, and was known through the years as not only a world-renowned evangelist but as a kind, non-judgmental, accepting and humorous soul. He was also, like Samuel, a man of great integrity who was never accused of financial impropriety. Graham famously said, "My home is in heaven. I'm just travelling through this world." I think the writer to the Hebrews would have approved.

The author then considers a great many people of faith together in one group: *the prophets*—a host of stellar figures such as Isaiah and Jeremiah and Ezekiel. The one who above all defines the role of the prophet is Elijah, in his confrontation with the prophets of Baal on Mount Carmel, declaring that God was turning Israel's hearts back to him (1 Kings 18 v 37). His ministry pointed to the one who would herald the arrival of God's Messiah (Malachi 4 v 5), a task fulfilled by John the Baptist, who preached repentance (turning to God) in preparation for the arrival of Christ. Indeed, God continues to bless us with preachers who call us with God's word to turn back to him. We can thank God for the ministries of preachers not just in the past—such as George Whitefield, Jonathan Edwards and Charles Spurgeon—but also for countless faithful local-church preachers today, as well as powerfully encouraging platform speakers like John Piper and Thabiti Anyabwile (available on The Gospel Coalition website, thegospelcoalition.org/videos).

The whole point of Hebrews 11 is this: as God has always empowered mighty victories though faith in him, so his people can believe great things of God and attempt great things for God... by faith in our great God today.

SOME GREAT ACCOMPLISHMENTS BY FAITH

In Hebrews 11 v 33, the author turns from *names* to *activities* empowered by faith in the Lord.

Solomon and Nehemiah "administered justice, and gained what was promised". Solomon began to reveal his God-given wisdom when he famously brought justice to a mother robbed of her child (1 Kings 3 v 16-28); soon the nations were coming to him for his wisdom, which we can still access today in the principles of Proverbs, the paradoxes of Ecclesiastes, and the passion of Song of Songs. Solomon was reigning in Israel when God's people finally "gained what was promised" and occupied all the land originally promised by the Lord.

Nehemiah, cupbearer to the Persian king, then unexpectedly promoted to be governor of Jerusalem in 546 BC, led the people to rebuild the walls of Jerusalem in just 52 days despite the cynical opposition of Sanballat and Tobias (Nehemiah 4); and he ended the unjust exploitation of the poor by the wealthy establishment. And God is still using his people by their faith to bring justice today. So, Christians in Parliament supports many members of the British Parliament in their faith and is active in working to protect freedom of speech in universities for gospel outreach, limiting office hours on Sundays to allow people to go to church, and battling to limit abortions so babies can grow up to hear the gospel.

By faith in the sovereignty of the Most High, in Babylon Daniel "shut the mouths of lions" when he continued openly to pray in defiance of the king's edict. When he was thrown into a den of lions, the Lord was with him to keep him safe (Daniel 6). His friends, Shadrach, Meshach and Abednego "quenched the fury of the flames, and escaped the edge of the sword" when the Lord preserved them in Nebuchadnezzar's fiery furnace (Daniel 3). Like them, believers in countries like Pakistan and China continue to worship God despite repressive governments.

For others, like Samson, their "weakness was turned to strength" or, like David, they became "powerful in battle and routed foreign armies". Still others, like the widow of Zarephath and the Shunammite woman, "received back their dead, raised to life again" when Elijah and Elisha prayed in faith for them (1 Kings 17 v 17-24, 2 Kings 4).

All these great victories were achieved "through faith" (Hebrews 11 v 33)—the confidence of these believers that God is powerful.

We can experience the same, not in conquering or defending the land of Israel—as Zionists do—for the land is fulfilled in Christ and his heavenly kingdom. But we "fight the good fight of the faith" (1 Timothy 6 v 12) by proclaiming the gospel and contending for the faith. We fight spiritually when we "demolish arguments and every pretension that sets itself up against the knowledge of God, and we take captive every thought to make it obedient to Christ" (2 Corinthians 10 v 5).

We can be bold to pray, and speak out, and write blogs and articles and books, and organise missions, and plant churches "by faith" in the gospel. We can have a go at difficult and frightening things that will advance the gospel, knowing that the outcome is in God's hands and that we have a chance of victory in his power.

Small groups of ordinary people have started new Co-Mission churches across London through such faith in God. A few of these church plants pushed hard but eventually had to be closed. A few plants are not growing numerically but are growing spiritually. Most of the plants are growing both spiritually and numerically—by God's grace and to his glory.

In my own life, while God has brought me and my family through times of sickness and hardship, he has also grown and multiplied our little church plant amazingly through our ordinary, faithful teaching of the Bible and the sacrificial service of his people—to God be all the praise. When we celebrated our church's 25-year jubilee, we commissioned our worship pastor, Michael Morrow, to write a beautiful song called, "Behold the power of his word", because we wanted to recognise that God has been powerfully at work among us through his word and we must praise him for it. The song includes these lyrics:

> There is salvation in his word:
> His voice has called us from the grave;
> I will trust his promise.
> We are surrounded by his grace
> Here in the midst of those he's saved;
> I will trust his promise.

Indeed in every church family, "we are surrounded by his grace, here in the midst of those he's saved", and it is right to praise God for accomplishing this through the persevering faith of his people. Hebrews 11 wants to remind us that God empowers his people by faith not only to suffer for the gospel but also to succeed for the gospel. We need to praise God for both.

Is there a gospel initiative you could join, and the only thing holding you back is fear of failure? Let Hebrews 11 encourage you to attempt great things for God by faith in our great God.

10. ENDURING

By faith we can endure horrendous things

There were others who were tortured, refusing to be released so that they might gain an even better resurrection. Some faced jeers and flogging, and even chains and imprisonment. They were put to death by stoning; they were sawn in two; they were killed by the sword. They went about in sheepskins and goatskins, destitute, persecuted and ill-treated—the world was not worthy of them. They wandered in deserts and mountains, living in caves and in holes in the ground.

(Hebrews 11 v 35-38)

I once visited an enormous church gathering in a cinema in central London. The praise band really was fantastic. The dancers were amazing, and the quality of presentation was exceptional. There was even an *X-Factor* TV celebrity on stage for the thanksgiving ceremony. But I came away disturbed by the message I heard. The impression was given that faith in Jesus inevitably brings success and prosperity. A video was shown of a South African couple whose baby had apparently been born with twisted legs but had been amazingly healed through prayer. The pastor read from a fistful of prayer requests from church members for better jobs, physical healing and new partners, and then he thrust the fistful of requests into the air and called on God to grant them all. There was a collection taken, and although the pastor said that God is not a slot machine for making money, he assured us that the more we gave, the more material blessings we would enjoy. The talk was brilliantly communicated. It summarised the message of the Bible as "God did good; we did bad; now God does good"—but there was no hint that God could ever expect us to face any hardship.

Please don't hear me as being enviously negative about a big church. There was a lot to admire. We surely should aspire to love people with the best quality of Sunday presentation we can provide to help people discover and grow in Christ. And we do want to be reminded of God's extravagant kindness to us in Jesus—and to celebrate him with joy! But I left that church with the impression that if we have faith in Christ, we will only experience health, wealth, happiness and success. This message is generally known as "the prosperity gospel". There's a lot of it in London and on the God Channel and in mega-churches of the USA, Africa and South Korea.

But what do Christians who are taught such expectations of faith do when, despite their desperate prayers, cancer takes a loved one, or they lose their job, or they discover they can't have children, or they face vicious criticism for their faith at work? After desperately trying to "have enough faith" that God will be persuaded to do what they ask, many will want to give up in despair, feeling disillusioned with God or guilty for failing to have enough faith, and often cast aside by a church claiming that real faith would bring success. I wonder if this is one reason why such churches collect the hopeful young but seem to lose disillusioned older people over time.

I once stood with a man crying by the bed of his dying wife, as he told me that some Christians had told him he was responsible for her death because he didn't have enough faith for her healing. I admit I wanted to punch them for such cruelty. Actually, Jesus and his apostles wouldn't have lasted long at such a "prosperity gospel" church because their faith brought them suffering and death! The author of Hebrews teaches his readers to expect not just success but also suffering—not only victory but victimisation too...

FAITH ENDURES VICTIMISATION

Some were tortured (Hebrews 11 v 35). But by faith in the future kingdom of God, they accepted it, "refusing to be released so that they might gain an even better resurrection", and so approved by God for ever. In the Maccabean Wars (167-160 BC), especially under the despot Antiochus, many faithful Jews had been cruelly crucified—as Christians were later rounded up by the Roman emperor Nero and burned as torches in his garden. Bishop Polycarp of Smyrna was dragged in his old age into a huge amphitheatre to deny Christ or be burned at the stake. He boldly cried, "For 86 years I have served Christ and he has done me no wrong. How then can I blaspheme my King, who saved me?" He was burned to death like many others.

It all sounds like a horror movie. But this is still reality for many of our brothers and sisters in Christ today. For example, Open Doors repeatedly report that in Eritrea it is common practice for Christians to be crammed into metal shipping containers for days in the desert in scorching heat. If God can empower people to endure such misery by faith, surely we can endure the embarrassment of inviting a neighbour to church.

By tradition, Jeremiah "faced jeers and flogging, and even chains and imprisonment"; and Zechariah was "put to death by stoning"; and Isaiah was "sawn in two" (Hebrews 11 v 36-37). So now, in even greater numbers, God's people are "destitute, persecuted and ill-treated" (v 37) in Oman, Pakistan, North Korea and Indonesia. In Cappadocia, in the centre of present-day Turkey, you can visit remote caves (decorated with Christian paintings) where many early Christians once fled to live, by faith, as primitive refugees "in sheepskins and goatskins ... in deserts and mountains, living in caves and in holes in the ground" (v 37-38).

Ever since Jesus, Christians have faced economic oppression, criticism, threats, arrest, beatings and sometimes death. While our founder's message is one of love—"For God so loved the world that he gave his one and only Son, that whoever believes in him shall not perish but have eternal life" (John 3 v 16) and "Love each other as I have loved you" (John 15 v 12)—it's reckoned that one in seven Christians (300 million) are suffering some kind of persecution today. Estimates of the number of Christians who have been killed worldwide over the last decade vary enormously from 90,000 a year (300 per day) to the more conservative Open Doors estimate—based on verifying that the motive was solely because of the victim's faith in Jesus—at 3-4,000 a year (10 per day). Christians are persecuted throughout the Middle East and increasingly in Myanmar, India, Pakistan, China, North Korea and Nigeria, and this is mostly driven by Islamic extremism or totalitarian cruelty.

On Easter Sunday in 2019, when the BBC reported the killing of 150 Christians by suicide bombers in three churches in Sri Lanka, the then Foreign Secretary, Jeremy Hunt, reported that the killing of Christians in places like northern Nigeria was reaching genocidal levels. Mr Hunt said that "political correctness" leading to people not wanting to be associated with the spread of Christianity by missionaries during the colonial period has played a part in the issue not being faced. "What we have forgotten in that atmosphere of political correctness," he said, 'is that actually the Christians that are being persecuted are some of the poorest people on the planet". We must pray that Boris Johnson, currently the British Prime Minister, does not forget his first Christmas message, in which he pledged to stand with Christians around the world to defend their right to practise their faith without fear of persecution.

WE FACE HOSTILITY IN THE WEST

While Christians in the West are unlikely to face physical persecution for being openly Christian, many of us are experiencing increasing levels of hostility. We face accusations that our faith is not just untrue or irrelevant but dangerous—particularly where it clashes with "woke" identity politics and sexual libertarianism.

We may face *scorn* if we talk about Jesus, *pity* for attending church, *rejection* if we invite someone to church, and "diversity training" if we express reservations about the latest LBGQTI ideology being promoted at work. "Freedom of speech" increasingly feels like an empty phrase, as our children are facing re-education by "muscular liberals" at school. Meanwhile, many Anglican bishops knowingly appoint practising homosexuals within their dioceses, virtue-signal support for political causes rather than preach the gospel, and divert resources away from evangelical ministries.

It has to be said that we do sometimes bring hostility from unbelievers upon ourselves. Sometimes we don't have an image problem but an integrity problem. In our personal relationships this may be because, contrary to the teachings of Jesus, we come across as *judgmental* (feeling obliged to comment self-righteously on the sins of others) or *hypocritical* (not really practising what we preach) or *disloyal* (treating people as projects and not friends). And our church institutions sometimes deserve criticism: for arguing about trivial issues while ordinary people suffer; for abusing power so that people have been bullied and abused; and for religious nonsense, when ceremonies and theological language have left people confused and alienated. It was Gandhi who, apparently having been turned away from Calcutta cathedral because he was neither white nor high-caste, famously said, "I'd be a Christian if it were not for Christians".

Yet there's something deeper going on. Christianity isn't the only faith with flawed people like us who make mistakes; and our gospel of grace and forgiveness and love is far more positive than most religious dogmas. So there's something deeper—something *spiritual*—going on in this hatred of Christians, which Jesus explained to his disciples in his last supper with them.

JESUS WAS PREPARING HIS DISCIPLES FOR HIS DEATH AND THEIR SUFFERING

[Jesus said,] "If the world hates you, keep in mind that it hated me first. If you belonged to the world, it would love you as its own. As it is, you do not belong to the world, but I have chosen you out of the world. That is why the world hates you." (John 15 v 18-19)

Jesus was preparing his disciples for his own persecution and for theirs. This is a vital warning for those considering becoming a Christian to count the cost before they commit—and for those of us who are already believers to manage our expectations and not be dismayed or frightened when we face hatred.

If the world hates you, keep in mind that it hated me first. The savage brutality Jesus faced in his final hours was truly shocking. The key principle when experiencing criticism or worse for following Jesus is to keep in mind, to remember, that the world first hated Jesus—because that will bring three helpful perspectives.

First, our opponents' problem is with Jesus, not us. He invented Christian morality, not us, so don't take it too personally.

Second, it's an honour and privilege to suffer with Jesus; and he will reward his faithful people in eternity.

Third, we need to respond humbly—to turn the other cheek—when we suffer ourselves, and to pray and speak up for our sisters and brothers facing hostility.

Jesus then explains two reasons why the world will always hate us...

FIRST REASON FOR HATRED: YOU NO LONGER BELONG TO THE WORLD

> If you belonged to the world, it would love you as its own. As it is, you do not belong to the world, but I have chosen you out of the world. That is why the world hates you.   (John 15 v 19)

We were all once part of the world in rebellion against our Creator. Our sinful hearts were naturally rebellious against God and his word. We didn't want to be accountable to God—we wanted to make our own rules! We didn't want to obey his moral guidelines—at best, so long as we didn't hurt anyone, we wanted to decide for ourselves what is right and wrong. But now God has chosen and called us out of this world. God will one day put down this disgraceful rebellion when he comes in wrath, but in mercy he has called many from all nations out of this rebellious world to himself; that's why the Greek word for church is *ek-klesia*, meaning "out-called".

So we seem like traitors to the world in rebellion; we no longer belong, and, try as we might to belong, the more we *behave* like Jesus and *think* like Jesus and *talk* like Jesus, the more different we seem—no longer part of the club! We're not necessarily socially different (we don't have to wear dull clothes and geeky haircuts) but morally different. We want to party but not like the world. We can enjoy good health and a nice house and a great holiday and the joy of family and career—but we're not devoted to them anymore because we've found someone better than all that. We used to make good things into "God things" and worship them sacrificially—but they can't satisfy or save our souls, and now we've found someone far better.

When I was a single man living in London, my flatmate John met Anne, the woman who would later become his wife. He suddenly seemed to get boring and wasn't any fun anymore. He dropped out of the bachelor's group of friends we were part of and wanted to spend all his time with Anne. He no longer belonged with us, and we quietly despised him for it. But then I started dating my wife, Sian, I was totally smitten, and I soon dropped out too.

Likewise, when Jesus captures your heart, you will want to spend more time with him and his people than with your old friends. They may resent you for it. And although you will want to maintain contact to try and have evangelistic conversations with them, they may start to exclude you, which can feel very hurtful. But remember, you've met someone *wonderful*. And he was often excluded too. And don't forget that you are part of an even more privileged club now: God's beloved family.

SECOND REASON FOR HATRED: THE WORLD HATES YOUR MASTER'S TEACHING

Remember what I told you: "A servant is not greater than his master." If they persecuted me, they will persecute you also.   (John 15 v 20)

No servant is greater than his master. We really can't expect to follow Jesus and yet avoid the opposition he faced. As we increasingly live by his teaching and defend his teaching, we will increasingly face the same reactions he did, and the division that was once caused by Christ will now be caused by his followers—initially the disciples and now us.

In general, Jesus' enemies admired his healing but hated his teaching. So today, people generally enjoy us being compassionate in our community but don't want the gospel that motivates us. People don't like Jesus' teaching in John 14 v 6 "I am the way and the truth and the life. No one comes to the Father except through me". It's too exclusive for the pluralism that people want to hear in order to avoid changing. (But if Jesus isn't the only way, then he isn't so special, and his people wouldn't be so motivated to be compassionate!)

So try as we might to avoid it, at some point, to some degree, we will be hated.

HONOUR IN HEAVEN

In God's eyes, this world is not worthy of his beloved, persecuted people. Though despised by unbelievers, his suffering people will be greatly honoured in heaven. In Hebrews 11 v 39, using climactic words that parallel verse 2, he says, "These were all commended for their faith".

Can you imagine the spectacular scenes of celebration in heaven when those who have suffered for Christ are presented to him? Such joy will surely make a World Cup victory parade seem pathetic by comparison. Many of us will live ordinary lives for Christ without much recognition in this world or even perhaps much appreciation in our church. But in heaven, our Lord will commend us with honours that will last for ever. It's not the big shots of this world—the celebrities and wealthy and powerful—who will matter in heaven, or even the famous church preachers who have had their rewards, but ordinary people who have lived sacrificially for Christ and have endured hatred for his gospel... by faith.

Now, astonishing though this is, hear why the faith of these martyrs has not yet been vindicated:

> None of them received what had been promised,
> since God had planned something better for us
> so that only together with us would they be made
> perfect.   (Hebrews 11 v 39-40)

Even such heroic faith was not then and is not yet fully rewarded.

God wanted to first send his Son to die and rise again, to bring his people from the past and from all nations together to be perfected in Christ, including us, and then to reward the faith he has created in us all together. So even now, their spirits are waiting with God: waiting for the great resurrection, when God will reward and glorify all his people together.

The writer clearly wants his readers to stop feeling sorry for themselves. It has always been hard for God's people. But since God has always empowered his people to persevere by faith, we can endure victimisation and continue evangelising our friends and neighbours and community.

Western culture has increasingly become a "victim" culture, in which people are tempted to compete in their complaints about how much they suffer. Western Christian are not immune to this trend. Of course, some Christians are trapped in terrible situations and need our compassionate care. But many of us will be humbled by this passage to complain a lot less and resolve to risk a lot more and endure a lot more for the gospel... by faith.

11. PERFECTED IN JESUS

By faith Jesus endured the cross, so fix your eyes on him

Therefore, since we are surrounded by such a great cloud of witnesses, let us throw off everything that hinders and the sin that so easily entangles. And let us run with perseverance the race marked out for us, fixing our eyes on Jesus, the pioneer and perfecter of faith. For the joy that was set before him he endured the cross, scorning its shame, and sat down at the right hand of the throne of God. Consider him who endured such opposition from sinners, so that you will not grow weary and lose heart.
(Hebrews 12 v 1-3)

I f you had to pick someone, who would you say you most admire? I mean someone who genuinely inspires you to aim higher. It could be someone close, like a parent or grandparent. Or someone who inspired you when you were younger, such as a captivating teacher or impressive youth-group leader? Or an incredible sports personality: perhaps Jessica Ennis-Hill, Usain Bolt, Lionel Messi,

Michael Jordan or Baroness Tanni Grey-Thompson? Or William Wallace, Nelson Mandela, Rosa Parks, Elizabeth Fry, Winston Churchill, Malala Yousafzai, Ada Lovelace or Albert Einstein? Sadly, many of our heroes are celebrated for a season and then crash and burn. Do you remember how Nobel Peace Prize winner Aung San Suu Kyi was venerated for her role in bringing independence to Myanmar? Tragically, she is now widely condemned for human-rights abuses against the Rohingya minority.

Of course, no mere human can ever be perfect or everything we admire, but even if we think of ourselves as pretty independent characters who grew out of childhood heroes a long time ago, there's usually a combination of people we'd love to be like: for myself I'd like to write like Sally Lloyd-Jones, preach like John Piper, play drums like Gordon Marshall, paint like Holman Hunt and look like Anthony Joshua! Well, I never said it had to be remotely possible.

There are so many people we could admire and want to emulate. The book of Hebrews tells us: *make your ultimate hero Jesus!*

KEEP RUNNING

As we've seen, the readers of Hebrews had once been courageous but were now weary of the hostility they faced and were tempted to fit into the world around them, like chameleons hiding from predators. The author has summarised their situation in chapter 10:

Remember those earlier days ... you endured in a great conflict ... publicly exposed to insult and persecution ... You suffered along with those in prison and joyfully accepted the confiscation of your property ... So do not throw away your confidence; it will be richly rewarded. *You need to persevere ...* we do not belong to those who *shrink back* ... but to those who have faith and are saved.   (Hebrews 10 v 32-39)

They were the spiritual equivalent of radiographer and elite runner Hayley Carruthers, who collapsed just before the end of the 2019 London Marathon and had to crawl on hands and knees over the finishing line.

Hebrews 11 has been an epic survey of characters from the Old Testament empowered by God to endure by faith to be confident in God's word (v 1-3), commended by God (v 4-7), obedient to God's call (v 8-12), patient in waiting for God's heavenly city (v 13-16), sacrificial for God (v 17-19), aspirational for life with God beyond the grave (v 20-22), courageous for God before governments (v 23), self-denying in joining God's people (v 24-29), empowered by God for achieving victories (v 30-35) and empowered by God for enduring victimisation (v 35-40).

Now this emotional rollercoaster reaches its climactic crescendo in Jesus:

Therefore, since we are surrounded by such a great cloud of witnesses, let us throw off everything that hinders and the sin that so easily entangles. And let us run with perseverance the race marked out for us, fixing our eyes on Jesus, the pioneer and perfecter of faith.   (Hebrews 12 v 1-2)

In the New Testament the comparison is often made between living the Christian life and running a race, which was a familiar feature of Roman life seen in big athletics competitions such as the Isthmian Games, and is also familiar to us from high-profile events like the London Marathon. Each comparison makes a slightly different point.

In *Acts 20*, Paul compares the importance of finishing his gospel ministry with an athlete's determination to finish a race: "My only aim is to finish the race and complete the task the Lord Jesus has given me—the task of testifying to the good news of God's grace" (20 v 24).

In *Galatians 2*, Paul compares his anxiety that the apostles in Jerusalem might have abandoned the gospel to a relay runner worrying that he'd finish his leg only to discover the other runners in his team were giving up. "I presented to them the gospel that I preach among the Gentiles. I wanted to be sure I was not running and had not been running my race in vain" (2 v 2).

In *Galatians 5*, Paul compares the infiltration of false teachers in a church to a runner being unfairly blocked by a competitor: "You were running a good race. Who cut in on you to keep you from obeying the truth?" (5 v 7).

In *1 Corinthians 9*, Paul compares the costly discipline of a believer living for Christ's reward in heaven to that of a runner accepting the pain of training to win a race. "Everyone who competes in the games goes into strict training. They do it to get a crown that will not last, but we do it to get a crown that will last for ever." (9 v 25).

And in *2 Timothy 4*, writing from prison, where he expects to be executed, Paul compares the satisfaction of serving Christ to the satisfaction of an athlete completing their event. "I have fought the good fight, I have finished the race, I have kept the faith." (4 v 7).

But here in Hebrews, the author uses the gutsy endurance of a distance runner to illustrate the gutsy endurance of a Christian who never gives up living by faith. "Let us run with perseverance the race marked out for us" (12 v 1).

At the end of Hebrews 11, having heard the "great cloud of witnesses" cheering the weary readers along, we read, "These [witnesses] were all commended for their faith, yet none of them received what had been promised". Because, "God had planned something better for us so that only together with us would they be made perfect" (11 v 40). The "something better" they have been waiting for is Jesus, who lived the ideal life for us by faith, perfecting and expanding all the aspects of faith described in God's people who lived before him. He lived the perfect life of faith for us, to qualify us for heaven—and now he is the ultimate example of what God can empower in his people by faith.

So in preparation for his concluding call—that we should run our race with our eyes fixed on the front-runner, Jesus, making him the hero we follow—our author clarifies three simple tactics for completing our race.

1. LET US THROW OFF EVERYTHING THAT HINDERS

Let us throw off everything that hinders and the sin that so easily entangles.   (Hebrews 12 v 1)

It's obvious that trying to run a race while carrying unnecessary baggage will make the whole experience more difficult and exhausting. In the 2019 London Marathon, in addition to the usual array of wonderful costumes worn by charity runners, one crazy man had a washing machine strapped to his back! That was always going to hurt.

Yet many of us are trying to live the Christian life carrying something like a washing machine on our backs. Including himself with his readers, the writer urges them to throw off everything that threatens to stop them completing the course...

a) Things that hinder

The word translated as "hinders" means "excess weight" or "burdens". What could they be?

Sometime a *toxic relationship* can hinder our progress in faith: perhaps materialistic friends who rubbish our efforts to be godly; or a cynical non-Christian parent who criticises our beliefs; or an unbelieving boyfriend or girlfriend; or a scornful colleague whose mockery is a discouraging burden. After prayer, perhaps with a Christian friend, in some cases we need to break off the friendship—or at least spend less time with that person. With family members there may need to be a respectful but frank conversation with a request to lay off. In our honest moments, painful though it is to admit it, we know that this relationship is slowing down our Christian growth and things can't carry on like this.

Sometimes our *ambitions* weigh us down: perhaps enslaving us with hours spent in the office or work brought home at weekends, and inhibiting our attendance at or involvement with our church. Desperately trying to improve our CV/resumé can prevent us from getting to church or midweek groups, and gradually we feel distant from our believing church family, and our faith goes cold. Can we choose to do less or ask the boss to let us go home earlier or do we actually need to look for another job? No one ever retires and says, "I wish I'd spent more time in the office", and no one ever arrives in front of Jesus on judgment day and says, "I wish I'd got further in my career"!

Sometimes it is *guilt for past sins* that cripples us with self-loathing, sapping any confidence and energy we might otherwise have used to get involved in a church ministry. We're like that soldier played by Robert de Niro in the classic film *The Mission*, who, having killed his brother in an argument, is carrying around on his back a massive, crippling sack full of armour representing his violent past. What joy when it was finally cut free. We need to drop our sackload of guilt at the foot of the cross by recognising that Jesus really has suffered on the cross the hell we deserve for all our sins. And we really are now beautiful and acceptable to God in Christ's beautiful Christian life. I've found that a good way to do this is to pray Psalm 51 on my face before God—and then I get up to resume my service of God, free for ever from guilt. Let's not increase the damage of sin in our past by allowing it to cripple our joy in the future; let's confess it, dump it before God and leave it behind. And then there are...

b) Sins that entangle

This means sin we find hard to get rid of. What sin is like this for you? Sin is always enslaving; it's a spiritual addiction. And when sin keeps tripping us up, radical action is required. We may be struggling with old-school addictions to alcohol, envy, gambling or pornography, or with currently widespread addictions to popularity, attention-seeking or self-pity—most likely a poisonous concoction unique to ourselves. In addition to repentant prayer, we will often need help from a Christian friend or pastor to break out of our sin because its hold upon us is vice-like. We like it, and yet we hate what it does to our relationship with God. So discussing it with a trusted friend or small-group leader can really help, so that we can agree some kind of strategy for displacing our love of sin with a greater love of God, supported by loving accountability. For entangling sin is like a boa constrictor. Tickling a python won't get rid of it—more radical action is required. So our author says…

c) Throw it off

Do something decisive to throw away that sin that trips you up while you have the will do the right thing (though be careful to be gentle where other innocent people are involved).

We're all recovering addicts when it comes to sin. So it's ok to admit that you're struggling and ask for help. You could say that being a sinner is like living in a filthy prison cell. In the darkness with so many others, we don't realise how filthy it is. But it *is* filthy. When Christ comes to save us, he opens the cell door and leads us out into the fresh air and sunshine of living by faith in a godly lifestyle of evangelistic holiness. But, perhaps when alcohol or weariness or self-righteousness or self-pity weakens our resistance, we crawl back into the cell and wallow around in our filth again. So Jesus patiently sends a brother or sister in Christ back into the cell to lead us out to the joy of obedience, where we belong. And one day, in death or when Christ returns, he will gently lead us out of that filthy cell to live with him for eternity, locking that dreadful cell door behind us for ever. What a happy day that will be!

Until then, let's get more aggressive with sin and treat it like a deadly snake. Stop stroking your sin and kill it, for "if by the Spirit you put to death the misdeeds of the body, you will live. For those who are led by the Spirit of God [in killing sin] are the children of God" (Romans 8 v 13-14). So the first tactic in this marathon of faith is obvious: *let us throw off everything that hinders.*

2. LET US RUN WITH PERSEVERANCE

And let us run with perseverance the race marked out for us.   (Hebrews 12 v 1)

Living by faith is not a sprint but a marathon. People who start must expect it to be hard; but, as with a marathon, we can all do it if we go at our own pace and refuse to give up. But we can't just lie on the ground.

a) We must run

It will require effort and determination. Sure, we are motivated and enabled by grace, but if we don't try, we won't get very far. When Paul says, "Work out your salvation with fear and trembling" (Philippians 2 v 12), he is telling us to work hard at our evangelistic holiness. Our Western culture is in general now afflicted with an angry, rights-oriented, "all must have prizes" approach to life. This can skew our understanding of God's grace. We demand the same experiences and outcomes as everyone else—and to just *be* and not have to *do* anything. But this is not biblical.

God is not only celebrated for being God, or even just for his marvellous attributes, but for what he has done in choosing, creating, ransoming, calling, regenerating, justifying, sanctifying, transforming, preserving and glorifying his people in Christ. He gives us all very different life-circumstances and gifts, and he alone will evaluate us fairly on judgment day. But Jesus' different versions of his parable of the talents or gold bags or minas (Matthew 25 v 14-30; Luke 19 v 11-27) makes it clear that while all his different servants will "share [their] master's happiness" in heaven, our additional rewards will vary according to how we have lived for him.

Jesus is looking for the opportunity to lavish additional blessings upon those who serve him well. His rewards will clearly not relate crudely to human measures. An unknown faithful Syrian refugee who has lost her husband to Islamic extremists, but who in her poverty remains holy and faithful in prayer, will surely enjoy being nearer to Jesus than the published and privileged Western church-planter who could have been so much more holy. How we live matters to God. He wants us to become more like Jesus *now* and not just leave it for heaven. God gives us incentives to run hard and not just walk—to do our best and not be lazy. Yes, we are saved by his grace, but his grace motivates and empowers effort and determination. This passage encourages us to run and not walk. Don't settle for average: *run*. And don't be surprised when it hurts. Just remember that the finish will make it all worthwhile!

b) We must run with perseverance

Paul writes, "If only for this life we have hope in Christ, we are of all people most to be pitied" (1 Corinthians 15 v 19). While knowing God makes every area of life better, there will be times when the present cost feels greater than present benefits—when the pain of being hated feels worse than the privilege of being hated. And, as in running a marathon, when the triumph of finishing helps the runners persevere, it is the reality of the glory to come that can keep us going. Paul writes:

> For our light and momentary troubles are achieving
> for us an eternal glory that far outweighs them all.
> So we fix our eyes not on what is seen, but on what
> is unseen, since what is seen is temporary, but what
> is unseen is eternal.   (2 Corinthians 4 v 17-18)

If Paul can describe his appalling persecutions—which he later says in 2 Corinthians 11 included beatings, floggings, shipwrecks, imprisonment and a stoning—as "light and momentary", how utterly wonderful is the glory to come? But we don't have to run anyone else's race...

c) The race marked out for us

We don't know if our life will involve cancer, humiliation or imprisonment. But it is a great comfort to know that our loving heavenly Father has designed it personally for us; we don't follow a course designed for someone else but the life designed for us to become like Jesus. For "in all things God works for the good of those who love him ... to be conformed to the image of his son" (Romans 8 v 28-29).

There is no other way for us to go but the way God has planned. We know he has designed it to be possible and given us his Spirit to sustain us. And our church family is running with us to encourage us; and the cloud of witnesses in the Bible is lining the route to bellow their encouragements and warnings from the pages of Scripture.

Living by faith is not just a race for elite athletes. Beginners need to run at a sustainable pace and not set off at the pace of an Olympic sprinter like Usain Bolt. New Christians sometimes attempt too much in their early enthusiasm and then crash in disappointment when they sin or burn out with exhaustion. Better, if possible, to settle in one good church (where the Bible is taught and obeyed, where we could bring friends to be saved, and where there are ministry opportunities for us to get involved in) and accept the guidance of more experienced believers.

But the third tactic is the most important of all for persevering by faith.

3. LET US FIX OUR EYES ON JESUS!

> ... fixing our eyes on Jesus, the pioneer and perfecter of faith. For the joy that was set before him he endured the cross, scorning its shame, and sat down at the right hand of the throne of God.
>
> (Hebrews 12 v 2)

a) Fixing our eyes

This means concentrating upon following Jesus because he is the champion believer to admire above all others. Amateur marathon runners shouldn't listen to the advice of inexperienced amateurs, and certainly not to the first-time charity runner staggering along in a rhino suit. If you really want to run the London Marathon, learn from Eliud Kipchoge from Kenya. He not only won the London Marathon for the fourth time in 2019 but later that year, in Vienna, broke the world record in the spectacular time of 1 hour, 59 minutes and 40 seconds—the first time anyone has broken the two-hour barrier. If you want to be a champion marathon runner, fix your eyes upon Kipchoge.

But if you want to live by faith, without shrinking back, fix your eyes on Jesus in the Bible. For he is...

b) The pioneer and perfecter of faith

Jesus is the *pioneer* of our faith because he has lived the life of faith before us as our leader and has now created a life of faith in us through the gospel.

And he is the *perfecter* of our faith because he is our King, who has completed a perfect life of faith for us, as our representative, by his trusting obedience to God's word, even to the point of death on a cross. It is his life of faith which is reckoned as ours to qualify us for heaven. And now he is training us to live by faith like him. The most important thing to learn from Jesus' faith is what he was motivated by...

c) The joy set before him

For the joy that was set before him he endured the cross, scorning its shame, and sat down at the right hand of the throne of God.   (Hebrews 12 v 2)

Jesus was motivated by his faith in God's promise of glory after crucifixion. He endured the pain and shame and is now reigning in spectacular glory. He blazed the trail—like Sir Edmund Hillary and Sherpa Tenzing Norgay blazing a trail up Mount Everest—demonstrating the way of faith for us. Sharing his glorious triumph is the future joy which can sustain us every step of the way; so...

LET US CONSIDER HIM

Consider him who endured such opposition from sinners, so that you will not grow weary and lose heart.   (Hebrews 12 v 3)

Consider Jesus everywhere in the Bible, starting with the Gospels. Listen to his teaching; obey his commands; watch his behaviour; learn from his decisions; and worship him! I don't just mean admire him from afar. I mean love him, worship him, pray to him, cherish him, depend on him and make him your ultimate inspiration, until your enjoyment of him gives you the strength to endure any hostility or discouragement you feel.

We need to beware the Sandemanian heresy which sometimes emerges among Bible-loving churches. Robert Sandeman was an 18th-century Scottish non-conformist theologian who overreacted to the charismatic emotionalism of his day by teaching that salvation comes from "bare belief in bare facts"— an entirely intellectual exercise. Faith is certainly reasonable and not unintellectual, but it is also much more. Thankfully, the Baptist theologian Andrew Fuller demonstrated from Scripture that saving faith is not just bare belief in the facts of the gospel but also involves delighting in the Saviour of whom this gospel is true—fixing our eyes upon him as our personal hero above all others.

God's word in Hebrews is telling us that if we fix our eyes on Jesus in the Bible, we will not grow weary and lose heart. If you fix your eyes upon Jesus, you can do this; like the cheering crowds of believers who have gone before, however hard it gets, you too can persevere, confident in God's gospel promise of heaven, confident in your unseen Saviour's loving care and living by faith for Jesus.

Fix your eyes upon Jesus
Look full in his wonderful face

For the things of earth will grow strangely dim
In the light of his glory and grace.

In fact, when you think about it, Jesus demonstrated all the characteristics of faith explored in Hebrews 11. He was *confident* in God's word in his preaching. He was *commended* for his faith at his baptism. He was *obedient* to his Father, even to death on a cross. He was *patient* with his accusers. He was *sacrificial* in his suffering for our sins. He was *aspirational* in welcoming children and in training disciples. He was *courageous* before the Sanhedrin. He was *self-denying* in his evangelistic ministry. He was *empowered* by his faith to pray constantly and to endure appalling injustice.

Faith is truly perfected in Jesus. So fix your eyes on him—and live by faith in him.

thegoodbook
C O M P A N Y

BIBLICAL | RELEVANT | ACCESSIBLE

At The Good Book Company, we are dedicated to helping Christians and local churches grow. We believe that God's growth process always starts with hearing clearly what he has said to us through his timeless word—the Bible.

Ever since we opened our doors in 1991, we have been striving to produce Bible-based resources that bring glory to God. We have grown to become an international provider of user-friendly resources to the Christian community, with believers of all backgrounds and denominations using our books, Bible studies, devotionals, evangelistic resources, and DVD-based courses.

We want to equip ordinary Christians to live for Christ day by day, and churches to grow in their knowledge of God, their love for one another, and the effectiveness of their outreach.

Call us for a discussion of your needs or visit one of our local websites for more information on the resources and services we provide.

Your friends at The Good Book Company

thegoodbook.com | thegoodbook.co.uk
thegoodbook.com.au | thegoodbook.co.nz
thegoodbook.co.in